New
Wilderness
Voices

5/6

New Wilderness Voices

* * *

COLLECTED ESSAYS

FROM

THE WATERMAN FUND

CONTEST

Edited by Christine Woodside

With a Foreword by Amy Seidl

UNIVERSITY PRESS OF NEW ENGLAND

HANOVER AND LONDON

University Press of New England

www.upne.com

© 2017 The Waterman Fund

All rights reserved

Manufactured in the United States of America

Designed by Eric M. Brooks

Typeset in Quadraat by Passumpsic Publishing

Paperback ISBN: 978-1-5126-0084-1

Ebook ISBN: 978-1-5126-0085-8

Library of Congress Cataloging-in-Publication Data available upon request.

5 4 3 2 1

Contents

Foreword * vii
AMY SEIDL

Introduction * xi
CHRISTINE WOODSIDE, ANNIE BELLEROSE,
AND BETHANY TAYLOR

Letter to Readers * xv
LAURA WATERMAN

1 Climate Change at the Top * 1
KIMBERLEY S. K. BEAL

2 Dark Night on Whitewall * 10
WILL KEMEZA

3 It's a Seasonal Life * 16
SALLY MANIKIAN

4 Looking Up * 29
SANDY STOTT

5 A Ritual Descent * 41
JEREMY LOEB

6 The Northeast's True Hundred-Mile Wilderness? * 54
RICK OUIMET

7 Hunting the Woolly Adelgid * 68
DIANNE FALLON

8 The Red Squirrel and the Second Law, or,
What the Caretaker Saw * 77
JONATHAN MINGLE

9 On Being Lost * 87
BLAIR BRAVERMAN

10 The Warp and Weft * 93
BETHANY TAYLOR

11 A Place for Everything * 99
KATHERINE DYKSTRA

12 Wilderness * 108
ANGELA ZUKOWSKI

13 Where the Trail Ends * 115
WENDY UNGAR

14 Catching a Fish * 124
LEAH TITCOMB

15 Epigoni, Revisited * 134
MICHAEL WEJCHERT

16 Steward's Story * 142
DEVON REYNOLDS

17 The Cage Canyon * 150
JENNY KELLY WAGNER

18 Walking with Our Faces to the Sun * 155
NANCY RICH

19 Getting Lost in a Familiar Part of the Woods * 166
AARON PICCIRILLO

20 One Tough Gal * 172
DOVE HENRY

21 Lady and the Camp * 180
ERICA BERRY

About the Contributors * 189

Foreword

* * *

AMY SEIDL

Her chest full of crisp air and inspiration, her feet firm atop
a forgettable mountain where the stars make you feel
insignificant and important all at once.
BEN MONTGOMERY, DESCRIBING THRU-HIKER
GRANDMA GATEWOOD IN *GRANDMA GATEWOOD'S WALK:*
THE INSPIRING STORY OF THE WOMAN WHO SAVED
THE APPALACHIAN TRAIL

I came to wilderness under the tutelage of parents who were captivated by the crisp air and granite peaks of the White Mountains. They, now eighty, like me, now fifty, brought their children into the wild to experience joy in nature, and to find, as John Muir did, "the clearest way into the Universe, through a forest wilderness." Picnics, M&Ms, and a night in a mountain hut were how my parents enticed us, and a timeworn photograph shows my siblings and me grinning in sweatshirts, happily mugging on the trail. We were eager hikers, cherishing the freedom of being outside all day. And while we couldn't articulate it at the time, we relished how the trail provided a potent contrast to our non-wild, stationary days. It still does.

The photograph, stamped with the date October 6, 1970, helps me relive my introduction to wilderness and my first memory of "the mountain": the pungent smell of leaves decomposing on a warm autumn day; the taste of cold water, dipped with a stainless steel cup into a singing brook; and the feel of my father's fingers, swung back like two burly roots, offering to carry me along.

Now, photos I've taken of my children join that photograph.

There they are, shimmying through Utah's slot canyons, walking among the sequoias, and cradling a delicate lady slipper flower. Captured in their faces is the freedom of being away. Perhaps they had just seen a waterfall and the dipper bird that nests beneath it. Or maybe it was the black bear that walked silently through our camp, so close that we saw the wrinkled gray pads of its paws. These are among the sights, smells, and sounds of wild nature now lodged in their memories.

The value of wilderness often passes like this from adult to child, yoking generations the way that planting rituals or holy sacraments do. That isn't the case for all. Grandma Gatewood, the legendary woman who thru-hiked the Appalachian Trail at age sixty-seven, found her way to wilderness on her own, because the complications and abuses of civilization compelled her to return to a simpler self.

I teach environmental studies to college students and each year see how wilderness draws young people in and offers to recalibrate their hurried lives. Many of my students can pull from childhood experiences like mine and return easily to the mountain, desert, or remote beach. For other students, outing clubs and field courses introduce them to wild nature. All of them find retreat and refuge, a quality of being otherwise unavailable to them when they are tethered to the routine compulsions of an electronic age.

In spring, as the last term papers are turned in, I hear about the adventures being planned and the excitement of juxtaposing the study of the environment with being in it, its crisp air and forgettable mountains. No longer slack from the long sit of an academic year, pairs and trios set out to hike Vermont's Long Trail, walking the spine of the Green Mountains from Massachusetts to Canada. Others venture into Maine's Hundred-Mile Wilderness, where they walk with the spirit of Grandma Gatewood in the near-primeval forest. Still others head west to the Colorado and John Muir Trails, where other legends like Gudy Gaskill hiked each summer well into their ninth decades. It does not matter which trail they choose, because they all seek the same thing: the physical and spiritual relief that comes when we've distanced ourselves from everyday concerns, when we match our breath with our footsteps and take in the natural world around us. It is our fortune that in those quiet but not silent spaces, individuals hear their own voices.

This anthology is a collection of those voices. Like other nature seekers, these writers wrestle with the timeless elements of darkness, coldness, and wind; challenge their bodies on ladders and talus slopes; and ultimately gain perspective on what it means to be alive in a complicated, changing world. Paradoxically, they find that their lives are simultaneously meaningful and meaningless when seen through the portal of wilderness. This is a strange but lasting comfort, a gift really. Wilderness not only transports us but offers a view, a lookout, on the relative importance of things.

Few of us can be in wilderness at all times. We live in the back-and-forth between wild nature and civilization. Yet when we are away from wilderness, we can listen to the voices of the writers gathered here, expressing what we too have found: our true selves, the importance of relationships, beauty, the finite and the infinite. These voices help us reconnect with our evolving perspective. They remind us of the universe we looked in on.

Being in wilderness is good fortune in our lives. It is more precious than anything we will ever own. *New Wilderness Voices* reminds us of this fortune and speaks for the community of people who value the good about living on this good earth.

Introduction

* * *

CHRISTINE WOODSIDE, ANNIE BELLEROSE,
AND BETHANY TAYLOR

On June 8, 2007, *Appalachia* journal editor Chris Woodside sat down
with her tuna sandwich at a picnic table set in a grove of pine trees
in Acadia National Park. It was the first day of an alpine research
conference that joined scientists, writers, and activists in the cause
of protecting the Northeast's fragile high-elevation landscapes.

Within a few moments, several people quietly surrounded her,
then sat down on both sides of the table. They looked at her intently, almost as if they wanted a bite of her sandwich, but in fact
they were about to ask if she would help them start an essay contest
for new writers.

The picnic-table caucus included Mary Margaret Sloan, Laura
Waterman, Doug Mayer, and Rebecca Oreskes, all dedicated moun-
tain people, and at the time all board members of the Waterman
Fund, a nonprofit that had formed to encourage preservation of the
Northeast's alpine areas.

Even before they were finished asking, Chris said yes, because
both she and the oldest publication of the Appalachian Mountain
Club make it their mission to help new writers articulate adventure and science to the public. But Chris insisted that the fund give
winners significant prize money, not just a few hundred dollars or
so. The fund graciously agreed and has paid $2,000 each year. At
first the total went to the winner, but later we awarded $500 of it to
runners-up. Such sums can truly help writers whose careers are just
getting started.

The contest, we believe, is unusual. We don't know of another
that encourages a dialogue on mountain wilderness. And it neatly

fits the goals of the Waterman Fund. Guy and Laura Waterman—whose careers reflecting on, writing about, and doing trail work in the Northeast's mountains inspired the fund's formation after Guy's death in 2000—were writers first.

The contest's mission is to encourage new and unique voices. We ask writers to reflect on the value of alpine lands without prompting them too rigidly. Because this kind of writing is so specialized, our field of entries usually numbers in the dozens, not the thousands. Many of our writers have spent long stretches of time in wild mountain lands, working or volunteering as opposed to merely moving through the mountains.

Although we did not set out to do this, we have nurtured a group of writers whose approaches differ from those of many outdoor journalists these days. Waterman contest essays lack the conquering, I-bagged-that-peak mentality. It's not that we dislike that sort of enjoyment. We have not specifically asked the participants to avoid talking about fun. But most of their writing reflects deeply on their experiences, describing much more than a good time had in the mountains. The essays here show a spirit of gentle awe for wild lands and wild animals.

During the first several contests, we asked for writing on any alpine subject. The results were some exciting personal reflections on climate change, backcountry caretaking, crowded ski slopes, invasive insects, the philosophy of being away or lost, and clashes with bears and wolves. Later contests asked for thoughts on technology and perceptions about men and women. In 2016, we asked for essays about the national parks and elected not to choose a winner; sometimes themes can limit the scope of writing. Watch watermanfund.org for details on future contests.

* * *

From that day at the picnic table onward, *Appalachia* journal and the Waterman Fund have solicited, read, and chosen winners and nota-

mostly women apparently

ble essays. We seek emerging writers, those whose words have yet to reach a wide audience. A number of our winners have gone on to publish more of their writing, in *Appalachia* and other magazines, and in their own books. We are proud of the work we've fostered.

The contest has succeeded in fulfilling its mission: new writers have received recognition, publication, and financial support while bringing fresh perspectives to the timeless issues of wilderness and wildness. In collecting these winning essays—along with a few others we thought too good not to include—we hope to celebrate how these writers have added to the lexicon of environmental writing.

This project came together thanks to the time, energy, and vision of many people. Without the commitment, financial support, and enthusiasm of the Waterman Fund Board of Directors, the contest could not have grown and flourished over the years.

Annie Bellerose, a teacher and writer, and Bethany Taylor, a 2011 co-winner, oversee the contest. Many others have joined us on the reading committee, including Carl Demrow, Peggy Dillon, Julia Goren, Michael Jones, Judy Marden, Doug Mayer, Rebecca Oreskes, Mary Margaret Sloan, Val Stori, Kim Votta, Laura Waterman, Michael Wejchert (a contest winner in 2012), and Chuck Wooster.

Neither the contest nor this book would have been possible without the partnership between *Appalachia* journal and those dedicated committee members. Our responsibility for identifying the winners, and for encouraging writers who haven't won to send more work to us, feels as if we serve in some rocky version of heaven. We have never found ourselves fighting, although some years the decisions have required hours of discussion. We champion new writers of all kinds, whether they are students, retirees, or somewhere in the middle.

We thank Stephen Hull, editor at the University Press of New England, who valued the concept of our book and has shepherded it through the publishing process with enthusiasm.

And, of course, we want to thank the writers themselves, both those in this collection and all those who cared enough about the beauty of wild mountains—and the threats to them—to put their feelings into words. There are so many writers trying out new ideas. We're delighted to be able to share some of their work with you here.

Letter to Readers

* * *

LAURA WATERMAN

The evolution of a land ethic is an intellectual
as well as emotional process.

ALDO LEOPOLD

The Waterman Fund is a key player and partner in the alpine stewardship of the Northeast. Since springing to life in 2000, the fund has awarded $175,000 in grants to projects that focus on the alpine zones and coastal mountains of Maine, the White Mountains of New Hampshire, the Green Mountains of Vermont, New York's Adirondacks, and the subalpine of Massachusetts's Mount Monadnock. Our reach extends up the Appalachian chain into eastern Canada, all the way to the high plateaus of Quebec's Monts Groulx.

High, rocky, and windswept, these above-treeline summits are among the most dramatic landscapes in North America. Their peaks rise above the surrounding valleys like an archipelago of islands amid the seemingly endless ocean of the Northern Forest. Few visitors to this stunning landscape come away unaffected. Indeed, for many who grew up here or have adopted the region, the very ideas of stewardship, environmental protection, and ethical responsibility are inextricably linked to these mountains of home.

The Waterman Fund's mission is to foster the spirit of wildness and strengthen the stewardship and understanding of the alpine areas of northeastern North America. We seek to conserve their ecological, cultural, and recreational values. We promote teaching, mountain trail rehabilitation, and scientific research.

Many of our Northeast mountains are within a day's drive of 100 million people. I imagine that most of those who reach a crowded

scary

peak consider the apparently unresolvable clash of wilderness preservation with heavy use. That does not absolve any of us from striving to resolve the problem, from doing the best we can to preserve the spirit of wildness.

The Waterman Fund was founded to expand upon the kind of stewardship my husband, Guy Waterman, and I practiced and wrote about. Maintaining the wildness of our mountains is at the heart of the fund's work. Philosopher and poet Wendell Berry has this to say about his recurring experience in going to the woods: "One has come into the presence of mystery. After all the trouble one has taken to be a modern man, one has come back under the spell of a primitive awe, wordless and humble."

In our work, we foster the possibilities for being awed and humbled, struck dumb by the mystery of alpine places. This intangible quality of wildness is threatened by our human urge to share: to build another hut, to put a new trail up a previously trail-less ridge to a summit that's already easily accessible. What happens to wildness then? That's the hard and essential question Guy and I asked ourselves, and one that those who work on the Waterman Fund continue to ask.

Guy and I were two people who loved the mountains, and we were writers. We shared with readers what we observed and learned about our own human impacts. Our first book, *Backwoods Ethics*, published in 1979, was reissued in a third edition with a new title, *The Green Guide to Low-Impact Hiking and Camping*, in 2016, with a foreword by Bill McKibben. *Wilderness Ethics: Preserving the Spirit of Wildness* was first published in 1993; its second edition appeared in 2014.

Guy died on Mount Lafayette in New Hampshire's White Mountains on a cold February day in 2000. His death had a reverberating impact on the people who knew and loved him and on those who read his books. Guy had asked us to evaluate the impact that our values have on our wilderness experience—even our environmentally conscious values. He wanted us to think deeply and ask ourselves the question: "What are we trying to preserve?"

Guy died convinced that the world had not heard our call to action. But within days of his death, two young friends came to me and asked how we could keep Guy's message alive. A third person, Peter Forbes, at that time with the Trust for Public Land, asked me how we could honor Guy. Our response was to create the Waterman Fund. Our idea was to make it possible for the hiking clubs and public agencies here in the Northeast to finance projects that focused on the alpine zone, projects which would ensure that those areas would be cared for, both ecologically and in spirit. The fund understood the economic reality of these government agencies and hiking clubs: their financial resources were limited, and the bulk of them were allocated to projects below treeline. We began to raise money and to spread the word that we would welcome grant requests for *alpine* projects. To that end, we asked that every project have an educational component, that it evaluate the project's impact on the spirit of wildness, and address the project's sustainability. We encouraged land managers to do their work with great care, protecting both the delicate environment and the human experience of wildness.

We supported, for example, New Hampshire's Whitefield School, which started a project for middle-school students to learn about low-impact hiking and camping, and the fragility of their local mountains. Our aim was to turn these students into stewards. Following our goal of encouraging trail rehabilitation, another early grant went to the Randolph Mountain Club, which wanted to mitigate the impact that hikers were having on alpine flora. The RMC hired a trail crew to work on Lowe's Path, first cut in 1875, from its entry in the alpine zone to the summit of Mount Adams. Educating passing hikers as to the necessity of this work—through conversations and signage—was a vital part of this project.

In recent years we have come to see how global climate change can impact the alpine zone. As temperatures rise, there is no higher ground for alpine flora and fauna to retreat to. We supported botanist Glen Mittelhauser in his work to inventory all the alpine and subalpine plants within Maine's Baxter State Park. Glen's team of field researchers documented 426 species in the park's eighteen mountains. Their further work will result in a field guide to the alpine plants of Maine.

The Waterman Fund is dedicated to encouraging the next generation to take up the torch, to turn a love for mountains into a desire to give back. We support the biennial Alpine Stewardship Gathering, which brings together researchers, trail maintainers, educators, managers, and volunteers, all with a concerned passion for the alpine zone. Each gathering takes place in a different region and is hosted by a local mountain club or organization. Our intent is to draw in young people, and scholarships are offered to make their attendance possible.

One recent outgrowth of the gathering has been a "wilderness panel," designed to foster informal discussions, especially among young people, about wilderness. We came to love the mountains through hiking their trails, reaching their summits, learning about their vegetation and rocks, seeking out their deep ravines, airy ridges, and rushing brooks. We encourage our future mountain stewards to ask and challenge others with the question that Guy and I asked ourselves: "What are we trying to preserve?" This question is as old as the beginning of civilized thought. Today, in the face of our fast-paced material lives, it feels more imperative, more urgent than ever to ask it.

There will always be pressures on the land. Climate change, which was not yet an issue when Guy and I were hiking and writing, is now front and center among the world's problems. Undeniably, there will be future impacts to challenge future generations. The Waterman Fund, whose object at the start was to support what

Guy and I believed in, will continue to move forward, encouraging the next generation of writers, thinkers, researchers, and conservationists.

The fund's essay contest has come to a joyful expression in this anthology. These fresh voices, the voices of those with boots on the mountains, remind me that caring for the land is vitally important, that it will take hard work, that we do it because we love it, and that we are all responsible.

New
Wilderness
Voices

1

Climate Change at the Top

* * *

KIMBERLEY S. K. BEAL

2008, Winner

 I am standing alone on a car-sized granite boulder, trying to see through the fog that walls off my view a dozen yards away. I feel isolated in a circumscribed world of white cloud and muted gray rock. Condensed water hangs in beads on a low bilberry bush. The wind is buffeting me so hard that I worry about twisting an ankle as I maneuver through this boulder-field, high above the valley. How long would it take someone to find me if I couldn't walk? Plenty of people will climb Katahdin today, but I am off-trail and not near a popular route. Despite it being August, I lose heat quickly and my hands are already creaky with cold. I hold a computer printout of a photograph, which flaps furiously and tries to get a free ride on a gust. I smooth the vital paper against my green pants and look again at the features of Witherle Ravine. There it all was in 1959: the ravine, the fir waves, and the cliffs. When I look up again the clouds have begun to dissipate and I can see farther downslope. Suddenly I'm blessing the wind as it blows clear my line of sight. Shafts of sun hit the trees and rocks as the whole world reveals itself in sky blue and forest green. For a moment I take in the miraculous sight, and then it's back to work. With a little rock scrambling I am standing in the same spot where the original photographer took this picture nearly fifty years ago. While cloud-shadows flow across the topography like leaves in a stream, I hold my breath, raise my own camera, and take the same picture.

This is just one of the innumerable memories I have from my first summer of field research on the effect of climate change at New England's treelines. I was trying to find out: would a warmer climate mean a shrinking alpine zone?

Given the harsh environment high on New England's mountains, it is rather a wonder that any trees grow at all. Indeed, above a certain height, trees become very sparse as the plant community switches to alpine tundra species only a few inches high. Tree species like balsam fir and black spruce do persist in scattered clumps, but they are trimmed back by the winter storms and take on a stunted bush-like form. They are called krummholz, a German word meaning "twisted wood." Debate exists as to what causes treeline—the elevation where trees give way to the alpine zone—but we know that different limiting factors are important at different treelines around the world. Climate is the main cause of treelines, specifically short growing seasons. In addition to temperature, other climactic factors fine-tune the location of treelines. In the Northeast, the effects of high winds, rime ice build-up and snow abrasion are thought to be especially important.[1] It is easy to observe that some locations in the tundra are "safer" than others for trees. A big boulder, for instance, may provide enough shelter in its lee for a fir to establish itself, but the tree will be unable to grow taller than the protection of the rock. There are also non-climate factors that can exert a degree of influence on treelines. These include cliffs (not even the mildest climate will allow a forest to grow on sheer rock), human impact (the effects of recreational impact around huts or hotels), and natural disturbance (such as an insect outbreak).

It is an amazing experience to spend time in this environment, especially alone—when the other-worldliness is most sensible. Krummholz "forests" are like no other woods. Lilliputian in scale, they smell strongly of soil, moss, and balsam. Moving through four- to seven-foot high krummholz is not easy. Branches that have fought hurricane-force winds to get where they are do not easily move aside. The boughs form a tight, almost impenetrable, canopy on the top and sides of a patch of trees, but the inside is dark and relatively clear. When navigating to a research site my strategy is to swim, not fight my way forward. The trees will damage me as much as I damage them if I push too hard. Instead I lean forward and feel for the path of least resistance. I am often reminded of a moment from C. S. Lewis's *The Lion, the Witch and the Wardrobe*. The children in the story push past some fir trees and find themselves in a new world. I never know what the inside of a given krummholz forest will be like but I always feel like I am separate from the rest of humanity when I am there. Popping my head above the canopy after an hour or two, I am actually surprised to see that the world is so extensive as to stretch over range after range of mountains! My research has exposed me to new aspects of the mountains and I feel I can appreciate them more deeply than I did before.

I often crawl on my belly, winding past the three-inch trunks of seventy-year-old trees. Having read historical accounts of brave pre-trail hikers, I know not to bring extra gear. The trees would grab any loose backpack strap or jacket, and I would not make it through tight spots. Adventure was greater in Victorian times, but I thank my lucky stars to be wearing Labonville pants instead of layers of wet wool skirts as I navigate the "thickets." Krummholz is usually wet. The needles efficiently collect water from the clouds and the sphagnum moss holds moisture exquisitely, making up the bulk of the "soil" these trees live on. In fact, the ground is often a pile of boulders or *felsenmeer* (sea of rocks) with the thinnest skin of humus above it. I have to move slowly and test each step to avoid putting my foot in a hidden five-foot hole. Even when I find this frustrating, I know my presence has a purpose.

Between 1906 and 2005, as the Intergovernmental Panel on Climate Change documented, the global temperature rose 1.33 degrees Fahrenheit. In that same period, treelines from Montana to Sweden rose in elevation. In other words, forests in many parts of the world are able to grow at higher altitudes than they did a century ago. Scientists believe that the milder climate of today allows trees to grow where only low-growing alpine species could survive previously.[2] Should we expect a rise in treeline in New England also? We do know that there has been a rise in temperature and change in many climatic variables in the last century. Surface temperatures in the northeast have climbed 1.75 degrees Fahrenheit, even more than the global average. Warming has accelerated in recent decades and winters have been warming faster than summers.[3] In Vermont, the altitudinal line between northern hardwood forest and boreal forest has already risen in elevation. Today the place where maples and beech give way to spruce and fir is higher up on mountains than it was in the 1960s.[4]

For trees that are limited by cold, warmer temperatures, especially longer growing seasons, should make growing easier. It is my goal to find out if trees in New England are growing higher on the mountains than they did one hundred years ago.

I first became interested in this topic when I worked as a naturalist in Appalachian Mountain Club huts in the Presidential Range. I had the precious opportunity then to live above treeline and observe at leisure that most striking of ecological boundaries. When I climbed the Valley Way or Ammonoosuc Ravine Trail I witnessed the changing life forms as I neared the summit. Tall balsam firs gave way to stunted krummholz and then to lawn-like sedges and miniature cushion plants. What is it, I wondered, that allows a tree seedling to sprout and proceed to live eighty or a hundred years in one spot, while a few feet away it cannot? The huts were also the first place I heard worries that global warming might cause this treeline to move up. My fascination with the alpine landscape led me to pursue answers in graduate school. At the University of Vermont Botany Department I have the freedom to find a gap in our knowledge of the natural world and try to fill it. I relish this opportunity to contribute to our understanding of the environment because it is comprehension that allows us to be good stewards.

I came full circle when I began my research. After some years in the mountains of the western United States, I came back to New England to follow up on my questions about this landscape. It was wonderful to stay in Madison and Lakes of the Clouds huts again and think back to when I worked there myself. On the practical side, these solid stone buildings provided a safe base camp from which to set out picture-hunting on sunny days or to cower in thunderstorms.

I knew that treelines in other regions had risen with temperature and that New England's temperature had climbed. I decided to find out whether our treelines also had risen and I needed a good way to measure change. Other researchers had used repeat historical photography (re-photography) with success.[5] If you want to see change in a landscape and you have old photographs of it, all you need to do is re-occupy the spot where the first photographer stood and take another picture. Simple photo-pairs of "then and now" allow analysis of things like erosion or human development as well as of vegetation change (for examples see the Landscape Change Program at www.uvm.edu/landscape). Though my focus is treeline elevation, the pictures I have taken tell the story of how the high huts changed shape and size through the years and also how fir waves move up mountain slopes. I can trace the paths of landslides and see how they have filled in with alders over time.

I played historian to find photographs, spending hours in the archives at the University of Vermont and the Appalachian Mountain Club. In their wonderful collections I found photographs, some over 140 years old, taken by amateurs and professionals. People were climbing these mountains and recording the views then as now. It was a joy to see happy outings of snowshoers in wool skirts or proud groups at the summit and know that folks still enjoy the hills that way. Enjoyment of the landscape may be much the same, but I was looking for a change in the forested background of those pictures. The long-gone hikers inadvertently recorded information about the state of the mountain at that point in time.

I found pictures of treeline from Mount Mansfield in Vermont, the White Mountains in New Hampshire, and Katahdin in Maine. Once the snow melted in spring 2007, I headed for the hills to track down the spots where those hikers had stood decades earlier. For my work I needed to be as exact as possible when relocating images in the field. Field copies of my chosen historical images were my guide, and past summers of hiking helped me to find the right general area to begin looking for the original location. I used the principle of parallax by changing my position until foreground objects, like boulders, lined up correctly with background objects, like summit ridges. The puzzle of finding the exact spot is addictive, something like a scavenger hunt for which I have to scamper from mountaintop to mountaintop, trying to take advantage of rare clear days.

As a researcher I constantly find my experience in the woods useful. Months of backpacking have taught me how to stay comfortable and safe in severe weather, but I have also gained scientific insight. The more time I spend in forests or on top of mountains, the better a sense I have of how the ecosystems are put together, which plants are most common, and what a "normal" state looks like. My undergraduate mentor, Dr. Joan Edwards, always stressed to me the importance of old-fashioned observation. In this era of remote sensing and computer models (which are excellent tools), it is important still to know an ecosystem on the ground. I think this familiarity provides a base from which to make realistic new hypotheses and interpret data. Each season in the field adds to that foundation.

Field seasons do come to an end, and autumn saw me back in Burlington with piles of photo-pairs to analyze. For every day in the field it seems to take weeks in the lab to process data and try to find the important results. I spent winter days in my university lab studying the photo-pairs while snow drifted down onto brick buildings outside. I may have been sitting in front of a computer all winter, but the images of the mountains in summertime reminded me why I was doing it. I used mapping software to resize digital copies of my new pictures to match the originals. Painstakingly, I searched for fixed objects (like cracks in rock) that I could locate in both images. I linked them together so that the two pictures overlapped exactly. I then matched the contrast and brightness to accurately compare the extent of tree coverage then and now.

I ended up with about seventy photo pairs that were of high-enough resolution to distinguish trees from rocks and tundra. Most of the historical images were taken in the early years of the twentieth century. Within each image I studied a slope that had uniform conditions (slope and aspect) and was distant from areas of known human impact. I also excluded landslides and avalanche chutes, which are a constantly changing aspect of steep areas. Zooming in on the area of interest, I flipped back and forth between the old and new images, noting the size of krummholz patches and areas where trees formed continuous canopy. I scored each picture for increase or decrease in tree cover.

Spring is coming again to New England and I am finally able to put some preliminary numbers on the trends I've been seeing in my three northern New England study sites. The more pictures I examine, the clearer the trend becomes. A majority of the 2007 photographs show more trees covering a larger area at treeline than their historical counterparts. Some images show no net change, but many of these are areas where treeline would not be expected to move as readily, such as areas with extremely steep slopes, which are forbidding to tree growth in any climate. Some slopes may also be more or less prone to vegetation change due to aspect. I hope to know soon with further analysis.

Increased tree cover after a century of warming is consistent with the hypothesis that warmer temperatures would cause higher treelines in the northeast. However, the complexity of both the causes of treeline and the changes in multiple climatic variables must be considered. As is often the case in science, these results will raise further questions.

With growing season expected to lengthen by 29 to 43 days in the next century,[6] we might expect high-altitude trees to be able to mature and cold-harden their needles, allowing them to survive more ice abrasion in the winter. Given that annual temperature is expected to increase 5.0 to 9.5 degrees Fahrenheit in the next century, should we expect treeline trees to be able to out-compete tundra plants for space? Alpine areas are effectively small sky islands in New England. If trees are more and more successful and invade into tundra, then the area of alpine zone will shrink ever smaller. Will slowly rising forest be yet another threat for plant species like dwarf cinquefoil, which lives nowhere else on earth? What will summits look like in another hundred years? It all depends on how trees respond to the changing climate of the Northeast and how long it takes them to react. After all, trees are long-lived and slow-growing so we expect some lag time in their reaction to change. Predicting the future gets trickier the farther out one tries to calculate, especially when the amount of warming that will occur depends on the gasses humanity decides to emit. Unforeseen circumstances, like the introduction of a devastating exotic insect, may turn the tables and reduce tree cover. Luckily the past is full of clues if we are willing to take the time to look for them. The more we can understand about how treeline has responded to climate in the past, the more we can say about how it will react in the future. The more we know about the ecosystems we love, the better we can care for them.

I've reached the summit of Katahdin on an August day that has become clear and bright, with distant lakes twinkling in the sun. There are thru-hikers finishing the Appalachian Trail, day hikers visiting from Europe—a few dozen people enjoying the view of Maine spread out below them like one big picnic blanket. In my mind I see even more people here. For me, the summit is crowded with the presence of climbers from many eras who came before and left records through their photographs. Their clothing looks strange but the expressions on their faces are familiar. At this point in the summer I have begun to realize that the view on which these hikers of the past looked down was different from the one I see today. The forest has been creeping slowly upwards since their time and I am here to investigate that change.

NOTES

1 See Peter J. Marchand, *North Woods, An Inside Look at the Nature of Forests in the Northeast* (Boston: Appalachian Mountain Club Books, 1987); and Kenneth D. Kimball and Douglas Weihrauch, "Alpine Vegetation Communities and the Alpine-Treeline Ecotone Boundary in New England as Biomonitors for Climate Change," USDA Forest Service Proceedings RMRS-P-15-VOL-3, 2000.

2 Leif Kullman, "Rapid Recent Range-Margin Rise of Tree and Shrub Species in the Swedish Scandes," *Journal of Ecology* 90: 68–77; and W. Roush, "Development of a Spatial Analysis Method Using Ground-Based Repeat Photography to Detect Changes in the Alpine Treeline Ecotone, Glacier National Park," *Arctic, Antarctic, and Alpine Research* 39.2 (May 2007): 297–308.

3 Union of Concerned Scientists, "The Changing Northeast Climate: Our Choices, Our Legacy," ucsusa.org/sites/default/files/legacy/assets/documents/global_warming/The-Changing-Northeast-Climate.pdf, 2006.

4 Brian Beckage, "A Rapid Upward Shift of a Forest Ecotone During 40 Years of Warming in the Green Mountains of Vermont," *Proceedings of the National Academy of Sciences of the United States of America* 105.11 (2008): 4197–202.

5 M. Sturm et al., "Increasing Shrub Abundance in the Arctic," *Nature* 411 (May 31, 2001): 546–47; and I. S. Munroe, "Estimates of Little Ice Age Climate Inferred Through Historical Rephotography, Northern Uinta Mountains, U.S.A.," *Arctic, Antarctic, and Alpine Research* 35.4 (2003): 489–98.

6 Union of Concerned Scientists, *Climate Change in the U.S. Northeast, A Report of the Northeast Climate Impacts Assessment* (Cambridge, Massachusetts: UCS Publications, 2006).

2

Dark Night on Whitewall

* * *

WILL KEMEZA

2008, Runner-up

It was mid-December. I don't know whether I woke in the wind-blast which sent the hut's turbine groaning, or whether I shivered myself awake. And I don't know how long I had been sitting there, on the ground, with my back against the hut's western wall, snow drifting over my legs. The weather was changing. Clouds frayed at their edges to expose sharp stars, and the wind had taken on a new voice. It was rolling downslope from the northwest and, hitting a house-sized outcropping of schist, drawing back for an unlikely moment before slamming down on the roof. It was like hearing a wave break underwater, like the timpani of your own pulse in your ear.

Despite the cold clarity of this north wind, I did not know how I had arrived at this predicament. My fingers were numb. I rolled my head to the right and saw that someone had vomited, and then I realized that it could only have been me. I hauled myself to my feet and opened the hut door with clumsy, ungloved hands. I pulled off my untied boots, struggled out of my clothes—wet and burning against skin where my body heat had melted snow—and climbed into my sleeping bag, zipping it up to my chin with my teeth.

I stayed in bed for the next three days. This may have been a bout with the flu or some kind of food poisoning. I retched far past emptiness, heaving up only the acid memory of food. I ran through miles of feverish dreams—slogging up fields of scree, where dim figures receded into mist upslope. Delirium and solitude made the hut otherworldly. Shadows danced on the walls. The creaking structure spoke. A man sat by my bed, reminding me to drink water. I'm sure that I imagined him—a fact which does not diminish my gratitude.

I had been eager for this winter caretaking job. Basic duties (hut upkeep and a welcome to winter travelers) aside, it meant the chance to live through the gray blaze of a White Mountain winter. I wanted to try on solitude, if only in the modest dose of several days each week. But the ascetic joy I'd read about in the pantheon of Wilderness Writing was elusive. Solitude did not bring clarity or release. The silence crowded around the hut, stifling as deep snow. I did not know what to do with the mineral stillness of those long hours. I felt like I was losing myself in the constant company of stone, snow, and fog, as if human companionship had been a lifelong illusion that was now stripped away, leaving behind the bedrock truth of isolation. I fought—and denied—my loneliness, and wondered whether something was wrong with me. If Thoreau and Muir could do it, why couldn't I? Respite came with weekend visitors, whose Sunday departure I would mourn.

Then there was the cold. The hut was fitted with a little black cast-iron woodstove. The supply of firewood was limited, however, and the stove—per the policy of my employers and rigid tradition both—was to be loaded and lit once each day, and only after sundown. I was unprepared for the cold's long siege, its indefatigable circling and prying.

The cold slid its fingers around the doors, up under the waist of my jacket, down the back of my neck, up through the floor, down from the rafters. Cold chased me into my sleeping bag at night and grabbed me each morning by the arm, as I sloughed the bag off. In this cold, I was a defender in the citadel of my body, forever ceding the outer battlements and earthworks, always pulling inward and further inward. This endless huddling, this constant reflex to protect the core, becomes a habit of mind as well as body.

Dark Night on Whitewall

With practice, the instinct to draw in can outmuscle the desire to reach out. I was becoming trapped in a kind of thermo-emotional sarcophagus. *easy now*

Then I got sick. After three delirious days in that sleeping bag, my fever broke. I could eat again, if warily. I was weak and tired. But I was desperate to get out of that sweat-soaked bag and out of the hut's haunting shadows. So, after waking up fever free and lolling around inside for a morning and into the afternoon, I pulled on my plastic mountaineering boots and walked out the door. I descended quickly from the porch down the trail, boot-skiing over the hard-packed snow and through the biting air. After the quick descent, I made my way down the side of the nearby notch along a wide, flat, windswept scar in the mountainside—a monument to the days of industrial logging. The sun was already trailing south and west behind a wall of mountains, and the light softening. I was craving consolation. I wanted to feel less alone in the world, and to have the world confirm that, in the grand scheme of things, all would be well. I wanted to feel exactly the way I had so often on top of a mountain. *better stick to the city!*

I have often wondered why I and so many others are drawn to mountain peaks. There is, no doubt, something about the physical exertion of a climb that releases a cascade of endorphins, sparks dormant synapses, and scrambles the workaday neural pathways. But you can get that running around the block. And this is not an explanation—just another way to describe the effect. So: why mountains? And why these mountains?

The stacked, totem-pole ecosystem of the northeastern mountains makes climbing a particular sensory experience. The ascension from hardwood to spruce-fir forest to krummholz to alpine zone, all over a rock-bound, root-snarled treadway, is its own kind of walking meditation. Hiking the trails of these glacier-scoured uplands, you pay attention to each footfall—but it is a loose attention. The intricacy of the physical task occupies the guard-dog of the conscious mind. Other thoughts are free to come and go through the mind's backcountry like flocks of crossbills through the firs. A rhythm emerges, following the percussion of lung, heart, and boot sole. The scope of your conscious attention constricts, as the high vault of maple, ash, and birch tightens, becoming the wet, dark tunnel of squat spruce and fir. Then, suddenly, you break through. Encountering treeline, the doors of perception are kicked open. Having grown accustomed to a visual world of several square feet, you are suddenly faced with hundreds of square miles, mind ranging across forests, ridgelines, and valley towns, and face to face with the fluid undulations of the sky. There is, in the hike of a northeastern alpine peak, a performative rebirth: a movement from dark enclosure toward a chilly, breezy rapture—and the embrasure of a wider, chancier world.

If I had ever felt the need for the ascension of spirit associated with a summit, it was that December afternoon. Knowing that it would take too long to trudge through drifted snow to a peak-bound trail, I decided to bushwhack. I turned to my left, to face the east wall of the notch. This was a small mountain, with a steep western face creased by shallow gullies. The summit was invisible from the trail, tucked behind the lip of the wall, overhung in several places by rock which had been undercut during the latest glacial retreat. Deep snow pooled near the base of the wall, but its angle was steep enough that there would be only a thin crust covering rock and ice higher up. With the weak sun falling west, shadows pooled in the gullies across the snow, marking possible lines of ascent. Facing the wall, I wished I'd brought crampons and ice tools. I had not. But I could see that, despite the wall's slope, spruce and fir hung on singly or in small bunches along the edge of a deep gully. I started up, looking for places where I could find some purchase, grab trees, and keep away from the hard tongues of blue ice. I climbed steadily, gracelessly. I kept my belly close to the sloping ground, clawing for every vertical foot. Past the midpoint of the climb, the trees became sparse. The snow crust was thin over the ice. I noticed that the stakes, if I should slip, were becoming high. I threw myself sideways over patches of ice, catching a fistful of branches just as I started to slide toward the rubble scattered a hundred feet below. Despite shaky legs, slow arms and little energy, the immediacy of the climb left little room for ruminations on cold, loneliness, sickness, or the sense of grave finality which had swooped in on me that December.

I hauled myself over the lip at the top of the slide, lightheaded with hunger and chilled by sweat. I looked east, the direction in which I'd been moving, up at familiar mountains: ice-glazed trees white against a flint-gray sky. Then I turned around, to look down the long valley. There, already obscuring the peaks at the southern end of the notch, was a towering wall of the darkest clouds I'd ever seen. The cloudbank was moving north and east, toward me. It moved slowly but with unflinching intent, like a slow flood or a black glacier on the march. It enveloped everything—the sky's fading light, the peaks, and the valley's trough. It was like seeing a negation, like watching the advance of absence. I had climbed that mountain with the last of my strength, looking for the solace of the peaks. Instead, in the gathering dark, I felt crushed by the full iron weight of winter. This time, there was no solace.

* * *

Wildness has a way of attacking our ideas about wildness—about its healing powers, about its place as a locus of easily accessible meaning. And this may be the final and greatest gift of mountain peaks. They remind us that the story isn't all about us. Mountains constitute an irruption in the landscape. They stick out, and they seem to have discrete points of origin and cessation. A mountain is a story with a clear narrative arc—unlike the undifferentiated sweep of steppe, forest, or open water. We are drawn in by the particularity of a mountain, its thusness, and its seeming singularity. But it is also clear with a little imagination that mountains are events: waves that rise and fall on a stony sea. As ocean waves express the fluid energy of wind and water, mountains make tangible the longer rhythms of uplift and subsidence, of self-organization and release. In this sense, they make tangible to us the immense forces which ground and surround all creation. Including us. And they remind us that the world will be what it will be—not what we want it to be.

On that cold mountain, facing those dark clouds, I felt neither solace nor comfort. I did feel, suddenly, the futility of my fight against the season. I had been trying to force the wild world to be what it was not; I wanted only flaring sunsets and major chords— not impersonal cold, or the forces of dissolution. On top of that mountain, I was forced into a surrender which was also an acknowledgment; the world must be taken as it is—darkness, cold, loneliness, and all. It was, and is, sufficient. More than sufficient. And, in that moment of surrender, I felt as fully alive as I ever have, before or since. Alive to the reality of the moment, alive to the nature of reality. The experience has stayed with me.

Later that winter, having made my peace with the season, I became a caretaker at a different hut. There, a fellow caretaker taught me the constellations of the winter sky. I would shuffle in circles around the ice of an alpine lake, leaning into the wind, face skyward, tracing the lines of old myths on the fathomless depths of space. I was aware that these stories were told to project human meaning into the void. I was glad for their company and for their humanity. But I was also aware of the darkness behind them, of the great trackless wilderness of the cosmos. I had learned that winter to be comfortable with that darkness: the wildness that surpasses human understanding, and which defies our aspirations for control. I had learned, too, to be even more grateful for places like the White Mountains, where the darkness still burns down through the light of human artifice, and the light cannot overcome it.

Dark Night on Whitewall

3

It's a Seasonal Life

* * *

SALLY MANIKIAN

2008

... we'll have no need to go searching
For the difference that sets an old phrase burning—
We'll hear it in the whispered argument of a churning
Or in the streets where the village boys are lurching.
And we'll hear it among decent men too
Who barrow dung in gardens under trees,
Wherever life pours ordinary plenty.

PATRICK KAVANAGH, "ADVENT"

 There was a time when I viewed heading into the woods for a caretaker stint as a big deal. I would stress over the little things I did and didn't have in my pack, fret about taking one last shower, and sign off my e-mails to friends as if I were departing for a wild expedition to the ends of the earth.

That view has changed. During the past two years as a caretaker —in cabins, huts, lodges, and canvas tents throughout the White Mountain National Forest—I've begun to take a more relaxed approach to my time in the woods. I don't measure out my oatmeal packets and coffee filters neurotically, or refuse hardback books because of extra weight, nor do I panic about what time I have to leave for my hike in. I look at the ground on the valley and the snow on the summits, gauge the heft of my pack, and a mental calculator starts clicking. This all is, most likely, because caretaking seems terribly normal to me now. With that normality have come systems of motor memory and (unconscious) checklists: an understanding of time expressed in footsteps. I've become comfortable.

Once I recognized my level of comfort, the ease with which I slide between frontcountry and backcountry and the degree to which I deny that there is a "between" at all, I began to consider the deeper development of a caretaker: how my relationship to my environment and my view of my job have shifted from the grand themes of difference and the exotic to a more subtle appreciation of the small. I have experienced a shift in self-perception; no longer the incredible caretaker, I am now someone who is just doing her job.

This shift was important and humbling and can be understood as "jaded in its best form." I might be ambivalent toward the uniqueness of my position, but I still retain a sense of wonder that I have been able to make an ordinary life in the national forest. Although a product of seven seasons spent in the woods as a caretaker, I fully acquired this wonder after my winter at Gray Knob.

One of my favorite places to look at the world is a viewpoint known as "the Quay," at the Randolph Mountain Club's Gray Knob on the shoulder of Mount Adams in the White Mountains. My mantra during my winter as a Gray Knob caretaker has been, "You can never go to the Quay too many times." I would veer off to the left when coming back from the Perch, swing by on my way up to Mount Adams, and often wander out just to see what was going on. The wintry white drama of Mount Jefferson's Castellated Ridge off to the left, the stripe of the rail trail down in the valley, and the edges of the Green Mountains rim the skyline in the distance.

There is always more to the story of that grand view. Seasonal change presents itself subtly. The waves of color in the fall start at the edges of the leaves of a mountain ash. Rime ice in October. And then warm sun begins to soften the frozen world of the alpine zone in January. The parade of birds becomes a crowded chorus by June. The first butterfly of the spring. The changing time the sun would rise—not just in the sky, but also over the edge of the cleft of Gray Knob—and arrive finally at the cabin.

These small things give motion to the vistas, bring the world of seasonal time close, close enough to touch as I peel the first frost off a mushroom, sink to my knees in new mud, and crack through the light layer of icing in the spring.

Vladimir Nabokov posited that "the poet feels everything that happens in one point of time." I think that, after a while, we all feel this to some extent when we're in the woods. Standing at the edge of the Quay, pausing in a moment, I always do.

It is a unique opportunity to be a caretaker for a season, and the luckier (or crazier) ones are fortunate enough to be caretakers in multiple seasons. In so doing, I have experienced weather and wilderness intimately, watched the progress of summer to fall to winter to spring and then back to summer once more. Along with seasonal change comes demographic change, from the crowds of summer to the thin trickle of the winter. And my own duties change: a fast-paced hectic summer day complements the ascetic survivalism of the winter.

In short, I have acquired an incredible sense of perspective. I have been humbled by my experience as a caretaker, by my independent forays into wilderness and my interactions with those I meet along the way. In this sense of humility is an appreciation of the subtle power of a caretaker, an understanding of the nature of stewardship. When I trace my caretaker self's development, I realize it ties directly to the path of the seasons and the ordinary mechanisms of living within them. With the summer as my introduction to caretaking, I moved into the next season and fell in love with the winter landscape.

There are those days, unfortunately now all too rare, that make a White Mountains summer. Dry clean air with a light breeze. Blue sky with puffy white clouds casting shadows on the rich green stretches of landscape. Bleached planks of bog bridges through alpine tundra, fields of lichen, berries, and laurel. Fluty thrushes, the purr of a junco, and the call of the white-throated sparrow.

Summer is a gateway into backcountry living. The weather is hospitable and soft, there are many people around, and one can move quickly along the trails. It is easier to settle into life and work when the list of lifestyle concerns is short, compared with the tireless minutiae of the winter (as will be shown later). For me, it was through summer seasons that I developed caretaker habits, and began my relationship with the backcountry.

There is a lot of work to be done in the summertime as a backcountry campsite caretaker. By eight o'clock every morning, I've begun my workday (my day began two hours before that with a cup of coffee and a book). I balance out my week by spending three to four days doing trail reconstruction or maintenance, two to three days working around the campsite, and one day hiking.

As a trail builder, I become obsessed with rock in the summertime. I tire visitors with conversations about rock, I harden my fingertips into calluses on rock, and I wrap my body around rock in a final desperate attempt to get it to move. I start to dream in terms of rock, about the motions necessary to move a rock from deep in the boreal forest brush to the treadway. I see the need for rock in washed-out sections of trail, I gaze appreciatively at beautifully engineered rock steps. I desire rock, the contact rubbing my skin raw on the undersides of my arms. Working alone as a caretaker, building trail, you are given time to know rock in a different way.

Evening sunlight through shaded spruce and reflecting green ferns brings the day to a close. With a cup of tea, I collect fees from hikers, filling out registration cards with hands cracked and dirty. When asked what I do all day, I roll up my sleeve to display the rock rash on the inside of my arms: "I build trail."

Although I seized upon trail building as the center of a backcountry caretaker's world, I do want to clarify something. Caretakers are not the same as trail crews, as we fill a different role in protecting the backcountry. Walking a section of trail with a friend of mine who has made a career out of that twenty-four-inch ribbon of a path, I became acutely aware of our different strengths as stewards. He is much more of a trail expert than I am, both at designing trail work and at moving big rocks. But I taught him the phrase "browse line." We each have much to learn from each other.

What it means to protect the land as a caretaker is evident in an exemplary primitive campsite that I once managed. Hardened tent pads take the place of platforms. The privy is a simple stainless steel bin underneath the outhouse. The site is set off the trail, hidden in a col. There is no shelter, no view, and no craggy summit beckoning.

Most important, there is no browse line, the measure of the distance of human impact. People "browse" the trees for firewood, and one judges the line by how far one can see into the woods. In many sites in the White Mountains, there is no privacy from one platform to the next because of the browse line.

Yet at this site, standing at one tent pad, you cannot see the other tent pad less than twenty feet away. Full-size trees grow into the site, plants line the edges of the roots in the paths, and there are actually spots of duff rather than exposed dirt and rocks. Humans have barely affected this site. It is a rare gem in the White Mountains' world of browse lines that extend for fifty feet, the ground worn away to mineral soil and root systems slowly destroyed. When I first saw this campsite, I felt the landscape, I felt the authority of the resource.

There is a spectrum of experiences: some campsites in woeful shape (the Mahoosucs' Full Goose), some examples of how things should be (this unnamed campsite), and others slowly returning through the persistent attempts of dedicated caretakers to rein in human wanderings through scree walls, revegetation projects (replanting trees), and visitor outreach.

When I spent a season as a roving caretaker through the Mahoosuc Range, just north of the White Mountains at the New Hampshire–Maine border, I did not do trail work. I moved no rocks and felled no trees. I composted hundreds of gallons of human waste from outhouses, mapped out a new campsite on the Grafton Loop Trail, and watched as the Appalachian Trail was relocated near Gentian Pond. I gained a strong sense of the role of the caretaker in contributing to the management of the backcountry and the protection of the resource in summertime work.

By mid-August, just when the summer season seems to have hit its stride, fall creeps into the world in chilly mornings and peaks standing sharp and clear against a blue sky. It is 35 degrees on the summit of Mount Washington one day, with a trace of snow. Goosebumps prickle my skin while I close my summer campsite down, tying tarps over barrels of tools in the rain. It is not long before that first frost freezes the valleys, and the first thick fog of rime forms on the summits.

Winter and summer are very different, but having lived through both and the seasons in between, I cannot see one without the other. During the long productive days of the summer, living is easy but the work is hard. I look forward to that productivity in the winter, when the living is hard and the work relatively easy. The shoulder seasons of fall and spring stand on their own, but also hold the promise of the next form of life: light dustings of snow and down vests in the mornings in October hearken February's tough dealings, and the warm sun and exposed skin of April are only the beginning of what's to come. As I write this now, with the summer season a hectic frenzy of activity and lush green heat, I feel nostalgic for the quiet trails, glorious white mountains, and blue skies of the winter.

The meteorological dynamics of the alpine zone, the ebb and flow of the snow pack, the accumulation of rime ice on trees and my jacket, the thaw and the solid flow of ice left in its wake—these are the elements of my winter. And these are the opportunities offered to a winter caretaker: the chance to experience wild winter wilderness closely, to learn the patterns, to build a relationship with the landscape.

I fell in love with winter alpine weather one particular week in December. On Monday, new snow fell the day I hiked in, crispy light snow that had me slipping and sliding into hidden spaces between rocks, bruising my shins and knees. Three inches balanced delicately on the thin limbs of the scrappy birches that eke out a living at the edge of timberline. My daily walk over to the Perch was quiet and calm.

Midweek the winds picked up, stripping the trees of snow and upsetting the balancing act I had witnessed earlier. Blown free of snow, the green spruce gave the illusion of melt. A closer look showed the "melted" fir and spruce covered in minute ice crystals, frosted with moisture wicked from the air. High winds and blowing snow shrouded the summits, and kept this winter caretaker mostly below timberline.

Friday came with freezing fog, cutting a profile of white among the trees and steadying the snow beneath my feet as it thickened with increased moisture. The firs around the cabin changed to white again, stiff with rime ice rather than soft cuddly snow.

As the winter moved on, the snowpack hardened and condensed with each cycle of thaw and freeze. Rocks became obscured; tramped-out trails become sidewalks. Wide expanses of snowfields developed above treeline. The edges of the rime-iced krummholz looked so sharp in the crystal perfection of a subzero day.

It started getting cold inside in December. I was slower leaving my sleeping bag, sighed with resignation when my water pots froze solid, and scraped hoarfrost off the windowsills to keep myself moving. While writing in my journal, my hand grew numb and stiff as I drew it along the chilled pages. I even chipped a tooth on a piece of frozen chocolate.

I maniacally scrambled to keep things from freezing: the gray-water bucket had to be dumped almost immediately, and water could never be left in the red jugs used to transport it from the spring. I traveled to chip the ice off the spring twice a day and was constantly carving away at the material in the outhouse.

Occasional cracks echoed in the main room as moisture gave way to ice. I thought of the stories of other winter caretakers: a cork popping out of a wine bottle with the report of a gunshot, the description of water freezing inside our own bodies in frostbite.

Yet even with all this cold, I never got more than chilled around the edges. Down in the valley, I was always shivering cold when I walked from a centrally heated house into the smack of 10 degrees Fahrenheit. The temperature differential between inside and outside at Gray Knob, usually not much more than 20 degrees, was conducive to acclimation.

I took a few adventurous hikes into the windy whiteness of winter. On December 6, my first subzero morning (it warmed to zero by midday), the day dawned mostly clear, but high winds whipped the new snow into ground blizzards. I decided to see how far I could get above treeline before I became too frustrated to continue. I sank into deep new snowdrifts, only to slip on ice the next step, and then scramble up bare rocks. Ice and snow seeped in through the zipper of my jacket and clung to my facemask. I almost lost a mitten in a strong gust while I was fixing my gaiter. I made it to one of the subpeaks, Adams 4, and then I'd had enough.

Later that evening on the nightly radio call, Bill Arnold commented, "Things looked pretty blustery up there today. Hope you didn't go out."

January 3 was my first full subzero day, and I decided to hike to the summit of Adams with my dog, Quid. Like most stupidly cold days, the sky was clear and the winds were high. Clouds of blowing snow misted the summits, swirled wildly around my legs and turned my black dog white. My body rocked with the wind long after I had returned to the haven of Gray Knob. My walk to the Perch was through a landscape of alpenglow.

On January 21, I said to myself, "Huh, it's a little chilly outside." It was 20 below.

Throughout the winter, I became aware of the many emotional pulls that the landscape had on me. I knew I could never live far away from such a place again, because days like January 29 would be missing.

I had no real plans that day. At least not until I heard the 7:00 a.m. weather report. After that I decided to walk to Mount Washington, for no particular reason other than it would be a beautiful day. Clear skies. Little to no wind. Trails mostly free of snow, alternating between ice, hardpack, and occasional rocks. A radical inversion meant it was 36 degrees at 4,370 feet, and only 6 degrees down in the valley. I hadn't been for a significant walk in a week or so, and was curious about the world south of Mount Jefferson. I looked at the dog and said, "Let's go get lunch at the Observatory."

At the Perch Path junction, I shed my hat, jacket, and mittens. I couldn't wait to reach the glow of light over the ridge at Edmands Col, where we paused for a sunlight break. Quid rolled in the grass and played puppylike among the humps of sedge. I looked to the spine of the Carters, reminded of the summer just past, when, from my work base on that ridge, I'd saluted the Presidentials from North Carter.

As always, it took a while to get around Jefferson, mostly because of the steep snowfields that awed me with their beauty. After passing little Clay, the summit buildings on Mount Washington loomed close, and my pace picked up. Water ice—clear ice that has formed from flowing water—was thick on the mountain, but Quid still wagged her tail as she walked behind me with a steady step.

Many friendly and familiar faces—both expected and unexpected—were at the Observatory that day. After I had raided the leftovers from the fridge (turkey! stuffing! chocolate cream pie!) and Quid had received a sound smack on the nose from the new cat, Marty, we headed back to our own neighborhood.

The clouds dropped soon after we left the summit. The snow began to fall as we passed across Monticello Lawn, pelting and pinching my face and crusting Quid's coat white on the windward side. And yet, when we made it back to Edmands Col, it was still warm enough for me to leave my hat in my pocket. On the Randolph Path, I could smell the cool melt in the damp fog. Wisps of moisture and clouds of weather surrounded Jefferson behind me. Drops and drips of melt and slush fell from the trees. I smelled the fragrant aroma of spruce. Snow fleas flecked my footprints on the Perch Path.

The mercury held high through the next morning, a damp and wet 40 degrees at 7:00 a.m. But, by the end of the day, it was back down to 10 degrees. I'd had a temporary window of thaw: a good day to be a caretaker.

I celebrated the leap-year day of February 29 with an "Adams Family Tour" over the subpeaks of Mount Adams: Adams 4 (I called it "Abigail" and it was renamed that later), Sammy, JQ, and then big ol' Adams himself. It was relatively cold by mercury standards (from 4 to 6 degrees), but there was no wind. I sat on the summit of Adams for almost an hour, just resting in the late winter sun. Quid stretched out beneath the summit sign, while I chose the view of the Carters and the Great Gulf from the rocks on the edge.

Spring brought an amazing thaw: a rapid change in the visual fields of terrain and topography. Every day revealed new patches of rock and ground, pieces of trash and, in time, a few blades of green grass. A tree I had snapped off the Perch Path on Sunday, because it was thwacking my knee, stood at chin level by Friday. Tiny Star Lake melted free, with the tinier Storm Lake close behind. Juncos jumped onto the patches of ground that appeared among the snow, and the trails became sheer flows of water ice.

Water rushed everywhere, roaring down Castle Ravine in a waterfall and forming a puddle on the Gulfside Trail. I grew especially fond of that waterfall. A kid staying over at the Perch caught me with my ear to the snow, smiling as I listened to the roar deep in the piled rock beneath.

A few nights of below-freezing temps would halt this mountain-wide flow into glazed melt on the snowfields and frozen drips on the trail. But this was only a momentary pause: the sun would come out the next day. Most winters are full of teasing temporary thaws, so when spring came, I reminded myself that this thaw was slightly more permanent.

With the departure of the prohibitive cold, inside and outside, the rigid schedule I held over the winter slackened a bit. I stopped scrambling maniacally to keep gray water from freezing. I exchanged my down booties for a pair of sneakers, and occasionally wandered around barefoot outside. Discarded layers of down and insulation cluttered the caretaker room, and I traded my insulated bibs for a pair of normal pants. My dog started shedding her under-coat—she was changing clothes too.

Longer days translated to fuller days. The warm weather had me ready to work, de-winterizing the cabins by removing the wood-stove and restacking the wood, and clearing downed trees off the trails. After the daily work was done, I would leave for long hikes over Adams and along the edge of the Great Gulf in the mid to late afternoon, no longer wary of a four-o'clock sunset. The living had become easy again.

One of the things I find fascinating as a caretaker is what transpires in that nexus between people and wilderness, how individuals, myself included, behave in and interact with the mountains. People come with so many different characteristics and habits, and from so many different backgrounds. One of the things one must accept about the Whites is the presence of people and, in my time here, I have come to enjoy the people who frequent these hills and the many ways in which they enjoy themselves.

To be a good hostess, a hospitable caretaker, one can't pull rank on visitors. I walk a fine line between making conversation and undercutting the experiences of others by imposing my own standards. This can be a challenge in the winter, when there is always a time when it has been colder, windier, or snowier (and I'm not just talking about my own experience). There is little room for dialogue when no one is allowed to feel comfortable.

For a winter caretaker who can recall the darkness of December and the deep cold of January, March is spring: balmy mid-teen temperatures, a warm strong sun, and a long stretch of daylight. However, for many people (eight Baltimore college students who have never been in the alpine zone in winter, for example) the world of March is formidable: blowing snow, breath-snatching winds, limited visibility, and persistent subzero wind-chills. An individual's understanding of signs and the signified is grasped through experience and memory; as a good caretaker, I refuse to force a hierarchy of standards into that shared realm of experience.

An additional challenge becomes demystifying the aura of a caretaker—the vision of a carefree life in the wild—while also retaining the subtle power of the position to command people's respect and thereby their attention. I expand on frequently asked questions to explain my job and to show that I am a person with practical duties and demands. I want to show the small in my own life.

In some ways, attempting to connect the minutiae of a caretaker's day with the grander image of an idealized lifestyle is just as important as connecting the small steps of seasonal change to the grander scale of mountain time. Branches of political theory and philosophy argue that the nature and direction of politics begin on a small scale, with an individual's self-understanding and minute actions. The personal is political; specific actions become tied to the broad scale of change.

Caretaking is a lifestyle composed of small things: the incremental changes you make in your own habits and routines to fit the changes in the landscape. You form a strong relationship with a place. It is a uniquely backcountry life.

But maybe I'm suggesting something a little more ambitious. In sharing these experiences, I'd like to think that I'm gesturing toward how something as unusual as caretaking is not completely unfathomable or alien. And, in a similar way, the backcountry of the national forest is not so unreachable either. Seasonal changes occur in the suburbs too. In describing the weather, the walks I went on, the minutiae of my day, and my interactions with those who wandered into my neighborhood, I'm trying to show that aspects of caretaking translate to life outside of the backcountry. These include patience, humility, and community. The authority of the land. A sense of self.

I am concerned about this partially because I am now at a point where I will be altering my own relationship with the backcountry, as I shift from full-time employee to a steward of a different kind. Yet I trust that what the backcountry changed in me is not bound to the ridges of rock and ice, the woods of birch and moss. Indeed, there already are aspects of caretaking that have wound their way into my life out of the backcountry. The small effects of seasonal change and human action, understandings produced in the nexus of people and wilderness in landscapes I have come to love, do not disappear so easily.

NOTE

The author expresses deep gratitude to Doireann Ansbro for alerting her to Patrick Kavanagh's poem, "Advent," which appears in Kavanagh's *Collected Poems* (New York: W. W. Norton, 1964), 70.

4

Looking Up

* * *

SANDY STOTT

2008

 This story arrives with the force of revelation on a windy, early-November Saturday in 2006 as I'm crossing the open, stone ridge that joins New Hampshire's Firescrew Mountain with Mount Cardigan. An early snow coats the mountains from 2,000 feet up. I am alone, as I often am in the hills, and I've left myself little extra time to complete this familiar, six-mile circuit before fall's long night begins. A flurry obscures the Franconias to the north, and slats of light paint Moosilauke's broad brow bright white against the dark sky. I'm focused on my footing. A slip and fracture here would probably mean a cold night out and, if lucky, a rescue, and in my summer shorts and fleece top, I'm prepared for neither. I've found a rhythm, and my boots are landing precisely. I'm reading the snow accurately—no slip-ups on hidden ice, each step a gain. I find my mind and body joining in a rhythmic dance of ascent. Like a face in a snowcloud, my father appears.

One hundred miles to the south, he is busy with his day: writing notes, making calls, working on behalf of one nonprofit outfit or another. At least I assume this usual day for him. But I also bear with me knowledge that here, in his eighty-ninth year, he has any number of medical fingers pointing at him. There is a balky heart, some dicey blood chemistry, and general gravity that weighs against such longevity. There are also two showstoppers: an inoperable abdominal aneurysm, first discovered during heart surgery four years ago and since tracked to its current unsustainable size; and a recently scanned tumor that has taken up residence on the business end of his pancreas. And so this visitation could be some sort of sky-sign that things are amiss to the south. But I don't harbor psychic ability or have much truck with it, and so, as I ramble along I am broadly happy with this visit. My father can't climb anymore, though we are only three years removed from an epic on Mount Madison, but from the time I was two years old, he has given me these hills, and so it seems natural that he would appear. What strikes me, though, is the clarity with which I see his gift to me. It ranges from my precise footwork over slanting rock to the foundation of optimism that still stokes each of his days. It is a gift given over time, across the thirty-one years that separate his generation from mine. It is a gift received slowly. It is a gift of the uplands worth exploring.

* * *

At some young age, those of us given the hills begin climbing solo to get away. There is, at that age, much to leave behind, a whole valley full of voices and expectations, a sort of broad version of the aptly named school torment, homework, wherein everyone seems eager to teach you the laborings of life and who you will be. None of us puts homework into a climb-away backpack, however; instead, next to the jam-soaked peanut butter sandwiches and candy bars, along with the water bottle and dry T-shirt, we slip in a knife, perhaps a compass and magnifying glass, maybe binoculars too. Tying your sneakers? Optional. "See ya," we sing to anyone within earshot even as the screen door swings shut with a single slam.

About a quarter of a mile later, the dirt road narrows to a few planks spanning a first stream. No cars can make this derelict crossing, and so the old road nosing into the hills grows grassy as it climbs fitfully toward the low point in the ridge where it tips toward the next town north. Whatever the destination—the high ledges and their scrambles, the beaver pond and its fat slap of warning tails, the cave and its rumored hermit—we feel a delicious singularity that is freedom. "Perhaps," we say, "this is who I'll be."

* * *

In this moment, I am twelve, still a newcomer to the valley and its two ridges (Skyland and Oregon) emanating like long, ropey arms from Cardigan and Firescrew's two-headed, central massif. These arms enclose a continent in my mind. The late July day is pancake-fueled and gilded with buttery sunlight. My father is already at work along the fringes of the field below the house, slashing at the new growth that edges out annually to reclaim our few open acres. Occasionally, I tease him about looking like Father Time as he wields the heavy-bladed brush-hook, a sort of upcountry scythe whose cumbersome swing he has yet to master. I have been given rare dispensation from my usual chore of hauling the pilgrim brush to a pile, which we will burn amid the new snowy wet of next Thanksgiving's weekend. As I step up Cream Hill's first inclines, my pack rattles the metallic samba of three empty coffee cans that are my exemption from a morning of dragging. The summer's berries are in but sparse in our fields, and already we know that a poor berry season below sometimes means a dense, clustered one along the Oregon Ridge. "Bring back the berries," said my father, concluding the unlikely deal forged at breakfast. This is my first solo to the ridge.

I am an athletic and somewhat timid boy, and already, as the woods close around me, I feel the frisson of this "wilderness" rubbing up against the stories of adventure and wildlife I've read and heard, a sort of mild electricity akin to that generated by grating one balloon against another. Snapped twigs make my hair stand up; dark coves of pine suggest portals; I weave a course along the faint line of our new trail to the ridge. Occasional pale blazes and scuffed leaves point the way, and I am good at spotting them. Fit and nervous, I am quick, breaking from the woods onto the early ledges only thirty minutes after leaving the house. These ledges, shelves for broad, shallow-rooted pitch pines and stunted oaks, also feature dense banks of blueberry bushes that colonize the fractures running through the glacier-cracked stone. A quick check beneath the small, glossy leaves reveals purple clusters of three and seven, berry numerics of a "good year." Begin picking here? Climb the remaining half-mile to the ridgeline and settle in there?

Berries with a view win out, and fifteen minutes later, I'm on the knee of rock that points east where the ridge drops off to forest. Fresh bear scat dyed a deep, iridescent purple says I'm in the right neighborhood for berries, and my own hair rises again. Stripping off my T-shirt, I turn to the work. Unlike my parents, my father especially, I am a "clean-picker," meaning I comb out the usual roughage of leaves, green berries, and twigs. My cans will hold small seas of deep blue only. At times, I single out particular berries of larger girth and special dusky color. I call them "fat-berries" and drop each singly into the can where they lodge like royals. Back humped to the sky, arms and legs moored to earth, I must look like some pale cub left to forage in this patch while his parents root about in the dark woods below. The morning sun lays a benevolent palm on my back, and the soft rattle of berries dropping into my can punctuates time, then carries it and the valley-world away.

* * *

Clipping on the plastic cover of can number three breaks the spell. I sit back in my final patch, absently eating berries, and look down on the patchwork of fields that angles along the river's course through our valley. At its end the stubby ridges pinch close, admitting only the river and the thin, dusty road by its side. Somehow, I am older and different, removed from the boy who left the valley. I consider what I know of the lowland lives strung out in six houses along the mile-long dirt track: first, in a lightless grove of hemlocks hard by the river and road is the vacation shack of the "Frenchman."

Jean Bois is tabbed as the valley bad-guy, chiefly for his habit of feeding booze to our single native, Carroll Akerman. When sober, Carroll, who lives with his wife, Mildred (the valley's former school-teacher), three houses and a half-mile uproad, is my father's woods tutor, wielding an ax with a precision and rhythm that sprays large chips, felling trees so truly that we have developed a simple game to test his accuracy. After selecting the tree to be felled, we place a can (in truth, often an empty beer can) on the ground some thirty or forty feet away at a point where Carroll says the tree will fall. Then we watch as the smooth, face-white wood-chips fly. When Carroll's tree crushes the can, as it often does, he wins a full one. I get the appeal of the game, of games in general; beer, however, is a mystery to me, as is the loud adult conversation that it greases. "J'sus Christ, Fred," Carroll will say as the two of them sit drinking companion-ably on the trunk of a felled tree, "ain't six people in town can swing this ax the way I can. I'll make you the seventh."

I shift in my ridge-seat, turn my gaze north. There, distinct even in the day's mild summer haze, above the rumpled quilt of country, are the pointy Franconias. Already, I have climbed along their soaring ridge a half-dozen times, but never alone. I decide that, just as I have come here alone, I will go there alone. And, though I know I will return from this first solo to my valley self and his worries about entering seventh grade and whether or not he will make the junior-high soccer team, I know also that some sliver of me is now of these high rocks, that he won't climb down. And I know further that I will begin to return to this ledge-self, to count him into the family of me.

* * *

I am seventeen, and, despite my nature, I've grown loud. Perhaps it is part of some plan that males reach maximum lung capac-ity when they have little of worth to say. Whatever the truth, I am loose in the Presidentials with five friends, and we are trudging and hallooing up out of Tuckerman Ravine with Mount Washington on our minds. In particular, we envision the summer crowds borne up by both Auto Road and the Cog Railway. Like many seventeen-year-olds, we both believe in and scoff at the heroic. Secretly, we see ourselves so cast, but we have devised a scene that undercuts this, plays it for irony and humor on the summit. Out of sight and a few hundred yards below this crest, I slip out of harness from my packboard and unrope a bundle of flattened cardboard boxes. With a roll of tape to secure them, I reassemble these boxes and then lash them to the board, tying in the whole ensemble with a final knot. When I shoulder my packboard, the empty boxes tower three feet over my head; I practice a few strides as if I were carrying another self. Now a reasonable facsimile of that White Mountain hero, the hutman (though the only nearby hut lies on the far side of the mountain), I head for the top of New England's tallest peak.

Washington's summit is a milling crowd of tourists, many of whom are bearing cameras, mostly Brownie Instamatics, but also some good, 35-millimeter jobs. Perfect. As we enter the crowds, my friends break out in understated celebration: "Nice going," one says to me. "Whoa," says another. "You must be exhausted." "What's going on?" asks an idle tourist, who has begun to lift his camera and find me in its viewer. "Well," says my friend, Joey, "he's just carried his body-weight up here from Pinkham. It's a rite of passage for guides-in-training." "No kidding," says the tourist, and he snaps off two photos of me as he calls his wife over. I smile and pose beneath my boxes; my friends surround me in various manic poses with flexed arms and jutting lower lips.

Later that day, I am looking down the north side of Mount Clay. My friend Ray waits a half-mile below me with my packboard and its re-stowed boxes. I study the glacier-split rocks, the whole jumbled slope, and then set off in a quick-stepping, high-kneed gait, dancing down the rocks, my feet landing faster than thought. My eyes are focused a few yards ahead; I don't look at my feet. Once, then again, when I sense there's a missing step, no steady landing, I leap high in the air, buying a few seconds to figure out what's next, and then I land on some edge, dance on over the gray stones, my boots knocking out their hurried cadence, the rocks sounding a hollow croak when my feet tip them together. In a few minutes I am down, chuffing air, my mind and legs alight with the fire of this solitary rock-dancing.

* * *

By my twenty-second year, I have burned through my first two cars, and now I approach the hills by hitching, selecting my trails via the lottery of drivers' destinations. One time, when a car deposits me at the foot of the Sawyer River Road, it's Carrigain; a few days later, I emerge near Lincoln, where I stick out my thumb again and ride south. Experience sorts my rides into three categories: the best (and smallest slice of the percentage pie) are the truckers and "regular" guys on their ways to work; the other two types divide nearly equally into those who want to lecture me about getting haircut and job (let's turn this hirsute vagabond around), and those who simply want me—I learn a polite non-listening and a direct "no"; I cultivate a faint menace as back-up.

The truck drops me at Appalachia's parking lot. In two minutes, I've stepped through the slot between trees, crossed the old railroad bed, and shifted uphill, away. Though I am solo as usual, I am aiming for the northern flank of the Presidentials, my father's old rambling grounds. Famously, in family, and faintly still in these hills, he was hutmaster, leader of the "croo" at the Mad House, Madison Hut, in 1939, and semi-adopted "son" of the North Country legend, Joe Dodge. Among Dodge's tribe of "Macs"—Red Mac, Green Mac, Sorry Mac—my father was simply "Mac," making him, perhaps, an ur-Mac. Anonymously, these thirty-one years later, I am here as part of an ongoing attempt on the peak of self, laying down a tracery of prints in the mud from last night's rainfall, climbing,

I hope, into an understanding of who I will be. I am fit and fast on the trails, hero of my own running narrative.

I've left behind the construction work from which I'm combing enough money to get by, and I've turned away from the law school applications that I filed for form's sake, just so I seemed to be applying to some future. All that lies to the south as I look up at the heaped, ice-split rock. The stones say little; I say little to those I pass. But here, on day three, is a moment: I'm dropping down into King Ravine to look for summer ice, and from some distance I can hear that I'm gaining on a gabble of voices. Usually, this is enough to turn me around or nudge me from the trail. Often, when I hear people nearing, I step a few yards off the trail and wait until they pass; few see me, even if I'm in the open. Perhaps it's the days alone, perhaps it's the high register of girls' voices, perhaps I'm simply lazy, but, as the voices grow louder, I stay on track to catch them.

The camp group, perhaps a dozen girls and two counselors, has halted for a water break; they're clustered on the narrow, steep trail. The canter of my boots alerts them to me some twenty yards above; I turn my feet loose. Usually, in the frozen posing of late adolescence (the state seems eternal) I would blow by them, but, as I drop down opposite the group, one says simply, "How do you do that?" I stop. "Do what?" I say. "Run down so easily," she answers. "We're killing ourselves to get down one step at a time; you're running." I look up. She's twelve or thirteen; her gaze is direct, curious; she stands forward a step from her peers, who giggle, which unsettles me. I sort through possible answers like playing cards—discard Paul Newman, ditto John Wayne, who can't walk; how would Redford answer? "I'll show you," I say, surprising myself, and then I search for the counselors and ask if that's OK.

For the next five minutes, I conduct a small clinic in rock-dancing, which depends upon maintaining a boot rhythm of quick, short steps, even if you have to dance in place before picking out your next landing spot. No big steps or leaps, no heavy landings;

it's all light and fast. I dance down ten easy yards, emphasizing the diminutive in my steps; I set up a faint soundtrack of short out-breathes. The girl launches, takes one too-large step, and then finds the little-step rhythm; she arrives with a wide smile. "Wow," she says, "that's fun." And inside me, an alignment slips into place. Of course, I don't know it then, but I've had an encounter with my life's work: teaching. Later that day, as I'm checking my map, deciding where to go next, I realize that I've been teaching this first lesson on the Chemin des Dames.

CLIMBING HOME

I'm not clear what awakens me, but the scene I see first is a slightly concave immensity of pale blue that bends beyond peripheral vision. A fine silk of cirrus could be the wisps of my dream's final image except that it stays steady, modifying the sky as I come free of sleep's long tunnel. I raise my head. Far to the east, Washington winks white above all its sibling ridges. I could be there, I figure, in two days, or I could settle back onto my stone pillow beneath this canopy of blue.

I can't recall exactly when I began my habit of taking naps during days in the mountains, but they are a very different kind of sleep from the usual shelter- or tent-centered slumber of an overnight. Whereas any sort of camping transforms place and time into a little settlement whose utensils and niceties have been lugged there in a backpack, mountain napping is the sleep of merger, it is the sleep from which you rise, in Henry Thoreau's phrasing, "everywhere at home." This tilt of feeling and practice takes place in my mid-twenties; by my mid-thirties, it is established. Now, I find that I climb not to get away, but to go home—to a region of best self, land-self, self-not-singular, upland-me, kin of rock, water seep, pine.

* * *

Often, I wake from a hill-nap as this self. Today, the tough, iced hide of March snow still covers the sun slope below the Oregon Ridge. I've made a chair of my old gut-strung snowshoes and, while my dog Wally snuffles and noses around the bases of beech trees, I lean back, close my eyes and feel the sun take my face and then my mind. Adrift in the play of warm air laced with fingers of cool I half-dream, my breathing slows. Finally, my mind quiets. Images and thoughts slide beneath the surface.

When I open my eyes, I'm looking up into the branches of hillside beeches. A cerulean sky fills the spaces between dark gray limbs. The sun has edged west to my right cheek. No wind stirs. Wally lies curled in a ball of sleep. My fingers play idly with his copper fur; he wakes, stretches. A squirrel emerges from a tree's trunk and climbs ten feet to a branch where it sits, tail curved. Wally watches too. The squirrel runs out along the branch and jumps into open air. I blink, straighten up. The tiny body hangs against the blue background, then begins to fall. A squirrel with a death wish? But the squirrel spreads its legs, and folds of skin unseen before form air-catching arcs; it soars downhill. Fifty yards on, heading for a smash-up with a trunk, it pulls its head up, neck bent nearly to its back, and stalls in mid-air, then settles onto sharp claws that clutch the tree.

In the afternoon sun, a whole troupe of squirrels emerges from beech homes and laces the trees together with the grammar of flight. Wally runs the ground from tree to tree, but they never fall.

* * *

Other times, it is some form of slow walking that brings me to this best self.

Yes, it was a good night. Snow fell throughout, a windless February snow, a full foot from a sky that broke into slats of early sun and now this near, blue canvas. Ten degrees only, but the labor of stamping upward on snowshoes and the late winter sun compensate. And I have reached midslope on the first wooded rise above Cream Hill, bound for the Oregon Ridge crest, rising slowly across an unmarred sheet of white. Each step is an act. I am in no hurry.

I lift my right shoe vertically from its print, shift weight to my left pole and lean forward to begin my next step. As I do so, I probe upslope with my right pole. I repeat, repeat again. The snow three feet to my right explodes. A whir of dark wings brushes by my right ear. Again a foot away. And again. No time has passed and it's over. I lean over my poles and stare at the three holes in the snow—three grouse had lain there asleep in sunlit snow caves, three fierce hearts beating slow dreams. I watch the wing-burst snow where they were.

HERE

Not long ago, on a work-blurred day at the high school where I teach, I was talking with one of my students. It was a rare day of strong winter sun, and under its close sky, we were looking ahead to summer, mulling over its possible trails. Escape is an enduring fantasy of schoolteachers and students alike. In winter, we are all in some way ungraduated, yearning for commencement.

But my student and I were also looking back to the past fall when we'd shared a classroom with fourteen others and read a gathering of writers selected for their loose kinship across time with Henry Thoreau. In that boxy room, we'd nosed through "Walking," Henry's forceful reminder that no day should be passed entirely indoors, that walking out into the world (his recipe calls for four foot-borne hours per day) is living and the surest connection to life's spirit.

Often enough, I hoped, my students and I had left indoor's fluorescence in favor of the clear and clarifying sky. With us, we had taken our hazed and work-addled consciousnesses, which I also hoped would not blind us to that sky. Outside, we had sought and awaited the moment where the squirrel runs its branches and leaps, mimics the best sentence structure and narrative surprise; the moment when sleeping thoughts burst fully feathered from the even snow of the given day. And in our meandering ways, we had searched for the land of the best self, the place where each of us could determine who she is or who he is. Those seemed good reasons for stepping outside where, even along the floodplain of the Sudbury River, it's possible to turn uphill. Some days, my student and I agreed, as we had climbed Henry's runged words and sorted our thoughts and tasks, we had awakened toward those best selves.

Each morning I emerge from my riverside house and look up. Above me, the same sky stretches its light north over the Oregon Ridge, above round-headed Moosilauke. I believe that the Franconias tickle its belly. I believe that Washington and the other pere-peaks survey their valleys from this same sky. All the years of looking up and climbing home have brought me here: to a place where each day I teach from the father-given hills, from their trails and viewpoints, where each day I am a guide. And on good days, perhaps I serve even as a sort of pater to exploration and thought that would locate good footing along the ridgy regions of the self.

5

A Ritual Descent

* * *

JEREMY LOEB

2009, Winner

> There was a lot of excitement up on the mountain
> yesterday. The summit broke their record temperature for the
> day with a high of 56 F (13 C), thousands of people flocked to
> Tuckerman Ravine, three human triggered avalanches occurred
> in the Bowl, people endured countless spectacular falls and
> several people were injured requiring lots of volunteers
> to evacuate their fellow mountain travelers. It was
> a classic day in Tuckerman Ravine.
>
> U.S. FOREST SERVICE, AVALANCHE ADVISORY
> FOR TUCKERMAN AND HUNTINGTON RAVINES, MOUNT
> WASHINGTON, NEW HAMPSHIRE, APRIL 26, 2009

 Halfway up the side of Tuckerman Ravine, on the eastern slope of Mount Washington, New Hampshire, I'm crouched in the lee of a cliff, sweating and shivering. My location, at the thin neck of an hourglass-shaped run named the Chute, affords a vertical view of the headwall. Blinding spring snow covers most of the broad cirque, interrupted only by dark cliffs and bands of ice, a waterfall bursting out from the snowpack and plunging into a crevasse near a center headwall run called The Lip, and the ant-like columns of skiers and snowboarders ascending the gullies. The exertion of booting up the steep face of the ravine soaks my face with sweat mingled with sunscreen, which seeps into my eyes. I shiver, not from the temperature drop in this shady spot, but from a gathering sense of danger. Tucks is rife with skiing accidents today, and I'm about to witness another.

A few days before, Mount Washington had caught a storm system that brought rain to the valley and over a full foot of snow at the summit. Winds at over 100 miles per hour churned through the ravine, loading gullies with snow and returning the mountain to full-on winter conditions. The blizzard departed as quickly as it had come, and this weekend beckons skiers with bluebird skies and balmy weather. By Saturday, the rangers have downgraded the avalanche forecast to "low" for all but the headwall, which they rate as "moderate."

I did not begin today anticipating avalanches, but from my perch, I have witnessed two major skier-initiated slab avalanches that rumbled down the headwall with deadly earnest. The second avalanche caught my breath, as a river of snow engulfed the snowboarder who set off the slide. He struggled to stay atop the churning rapids as they swept him 500 vertical feet, where he arrived at the floor of the ravine alive, unburied, pumping his fists in the air triumphantly to the roar of the crowd.

Avalanches aside, the slopes today are a mess of hazards and accidents. Novice skiers and riders follow each other over the edge like lemmings. Accustomed to neither the corn and mashed-potatoes conditions of spring snow nor techniques for descending steep terrain, they lose their balance, tumbling and bouncing like rag dolls down the steeps. Somehow, with disregard to physics and human anatomy, no skiers have seemed to seriously injure themselves. Across the headwall, tremendous blocks of ice that adorn the cliffs are melting imperceptibly, ready at any moment to set loose and crash into the crowds below. Deepening crevasses lurk around the center of the headwall, hidden beneath the fresh snowfall and waiting to swallow reckless skiers. Woe to the incautious.

That morning a friend and I had skied down the summit cone and dropped into the run called Right Gully, a 35-degree pitch. He skillfully carved the run, while I followed with adolescent audacity, my jump turns barely retaining control. Halfway up the Chute, the incline of the slope rises from approximately 35 to 50 degrees, and I cave to my fear and urge for self-preservation. (For reference, expert runs at ski areas top out in the low 30-degree range. Kickstep your way up a 50-degree slope, and you're climbing a ladder of snow.) Climbing such precipitous faces belongs in the realm of technical mountaineering—except for the fact that no sane mountaineer would try this without a rope, crampons, and ice picks. At 50 degrees—the maximum pitch for approximately half the runs at Tucks—you become airborne between your jump turns, and if you lose your balance, you have virtually no chance of arresting your slide. Such extreme skiing requires a polished, aggressive stance. For the skiers tumbling down the Chute, there's little to do but cover your head and pray that you don't bounce into the band of cliffs to your right or tumble off the ledges to your left. Heights and exposure do not usually bother me, but on the steeps of Tuckerman Ravine, I feel an acute sense of vertigo. Skiing here feels like willfully plunging into the maw of some malicious mountain god that waits to swallow its victims alive.

Daunted by the increasing pitch, and having run out of water besides, I choose to stop at this halfway point to film my buddy's descent. He's a much more agile, aggressive skier than I, and we're comfortable with this arrangement. I squint upslope through my camera, filming a succession of skiers, any of which might be my friend. The majority of them maintain control of their edges, cutting the snow with skill and quickness. Every third or fourth skier, however, tumbles and slides through the notch of the Chute like a race car spinning out of control, their skis, poles, goggles, gloves, and clothing tearing off and scattering. With every display of ragdoll acrobatics, a roar comes up from the crowd lounging on the rocks below, offering much kudos and empathy. After the skiers' tumbles finally halt, they pick themselves up, assess their wounds and squint upward to where their gear lays scattered hundreds of feet above.

At that auspicious moment, my camera shuts off and I start fussing with the batteries, so I only half-notice my buddy tumble past me, no longer attached to his skis. From the corner of my eye, I see a snowball of blue Gore-Tex streaking downhill, uselessly trying to grab onto the slope. He reaches the bottom, and I wait for him to stand up and give the camera a victory wave. Instead, he lies on his side in a crumpled fetal position, moaning. Moments like these feel surreal, where a wave of possible dilemmas and unforeseen consequences are suddenly manifest. I feel as if the wind has been knocked out of me; I can feel my adrenaline surge and my blood pound. "Just ski down there and check on him," I tell myself. "Don't panic until you have to."

As I strap on my bindings, somebody below cries, "Medic!" Of the thousands of people who have hiked Tucks today, and the hundreds who have crashed their way down the slopes, this is the first real injury I have witnessed. By the time I ski down, U.S. Forest Service rangers and volunteers have arrived at his side and are examining his left leg. We first note the dislocated patella on his bruised and swelling knee, but it takes a few moments for us to realize that his quadriceps muscle has twisted grotesquely, suggesting a fractured femur. The femur happens to lie dangerously close to the femoral artery, the main supplier of blood for the lower body. If the jagged edge of a fracture ruptures that line, massive internal bleeding ensues. If fatty tissue seeps into the bloodstream, it risks forming a blood clot that could lodge itself fatally in the brain or the heart. I forget about my dehydration and my clammy clothes. My fear and nausea disappear. I now devote all my attention to helping my friend get down alive.

Somewhere in those stretched-out seconds, two thoughts resound through my mind. First, that we are idiots who underestimate this mountain. It's been said often that there are two types of people who ski Tucks: those who are foolish and injure themselves, and those who are foolish and have the time of their lives. Which brings me to my second thought: Why on earth is skiing Tucks worth risking our lives?

TUCKS AS WILDERNESS EXPERIENCE

That question gnaws on me long after rescuers carry my buddy on a sled down to the valley and load him into the ambulance. What is so precious that draws us to join in this madness, this blatant peril and excitement that is Tuckerman Ravine?

It's tempting to reduce this type of extreme sport to an adrenaline rush, the sensation of being totally alive in the face of danger. But skiing at Tucks also partakes of a much grander tradition of high adventure in wild places. In a century where most of the world's frontiers have been mapped, traveled, settled, or paved, we have come to seek adventure in those places that can never be domesticated by man, the far corners of the earth that still hold us in their power. The more perilous these places, the more seductive their allure. Like high-altitude mountaineering or big-wave surfing, skiing Tucks offers a taste of wild nature at its most extreme, beautiful, and deadly.

If you ask skiers why they ski at Tuckerman Ravine, you'll likely hear echoes from across the past few centuries of wilderness philosophy. The concept of wilderness and its evolution in American history has been vividly documented in Roderick Nash's seminal classic, *Wilderness and the American Mind* (Yale University Press, 2001). The wilderness once held negative connotations in the minds of early Americans, who saw it as a place of chaos and darkness beyond the order of civilization. As the American frontier began to close in the nineteenth century, that sense of fear gave way to appreciation and nostalgia. Romantic and transcendentalist thinkers like Henry David Thoreau and John Muir led the way in persuading the public to see an American asset in the wilderness, its monuments symbols of our nation and its unspoiled condition as a natural cathedral. In the twentieth century, writers like Aldo Leopold and Rachel Carson popularized for Americans the principles of ecology, which demonstrate that man lives not above nature but within its web. In the 1960s and 1970s, seeking wilderness became a countercultural pursuit, a way to escape undesirable civilization and find a greater reality. Today, wilderness recreation has become widely woven into the complex tapestry of American culture.

When I asked fellow skiers about what drew them to Tuckerman Ravine, their responses echoed the classic tenets of wilderness philosophy. Many come to the mountains for that sense of rugged individualism that allegedly disappeared along with the frontier. Others are here to find the divine that has been lost in the confines of civilization, or to gain connectedness with the land, to shake off that sense of alienation that comes with a modern, consumerist lifestyle. At Tucks, surely, they invoke, experience, and appreciate many of these classic wilderness values. To carve a graceful arc down the side of a rugged backcountry slope is perhaps to touch the very essence of individualism, divinity, and connection to the earth. Yet Tucks is not a pristine wilderness area but the site of a long, colorful history of human recreation.

Skiers have traveled to Tucks in hordes since as long ago as the 1930s, when trail building and the introduction of a transportation infrastructure made access possible for weekend jaunts from as far away as Boston. Since then, on sunny spring days, the ravine has invited a constant crowd, what looks like a conga line from Pinkham Notch up to the top of the ravine. Skiers, snowboarders, and climbers mill around Hermit Lake, where the U.S. Forest Service posts daily assessments of the ravine's conditions. These postings describe in intricate detail the dynamics of snow conditions in the ravine. They always include strong notes of caution but stop short of expressly forbidding travel. This warning system seems to be a laissez-faire style of risk management when compared to earlier decades, when the Forest Service would shoot down dangerous avalanches and ice formations or close the ravine whenever they found conditions too dangerous. Nevertheless, it's a heavily patrolled area with multiple rangers on hand to educate visitors and to coordinate medical situations. For all of Tuckerman's natural beauty, the ambiance during the spring ski season feels less like wilderness and more like a bustling arena.

Wilderness, as the classic formulation goes, ought to be a place in the natural world where man is but a visitor. Not a place where man can buy a Snickers bar and some sunscreen, use the public restroom, or check his Blackberry, all of which skiers can do easily at Hermit Lake near the floor of the ravine. The Northeast has its contingent of writers and activists who feel the impinging crush of humanity sapping the wildness of these hills. Whether it's the system of backcountry huts, the overreliance on search-and-rescue, the crowded summer summits with hikers yapping on their cell phones, or insensitive visitors trampling delicate alpine plants, wilderness and wildness are under siege in the White Mountains. Tuckerman Ravine, the most traveled part of the most developed mountain in New England, could be the poster child for this debate over wilderness ethics. By most classic measures, Tucks represents not the epitome but the degeneration of the wilderness experience.

Yet in the past few decades, a new vein of environmentalist thought has emerged. It seeks to relocate the experience of wilderness as an inner attitude, not an outer environment. In his persuasive essay, "The Trouble with Wilderness," William Cronon argues that by creating a duality between civilization and wilderness, Americans define the latter as a place that spoils with any human contact.[1] The American imagination thereby allows for no middle ground where humans might live within wilderness, using its resources but respecting and preserving its integrity. Cronon suggests that with a reorientation of our concept of wilderness we can find it in the most unlikely places, even in our backyards. The poet Gary Snyder goes even further, positing that the power of wilderness is an intrinsic quality of being, not an extrinsic landscape: "A person with a clear heart and open mind can experience the wilderness anywhere on earth. It is a quality of one's own consciousness."[2]

If we believe Cronon and Snyder, Tucks remains an effective wilderness because its challenge and danger allow us to access the wildness in our hearts, to confront the unknown inside ourselves, and to develop our own inner strength in the face of chaos and confusion. Viewed this way, mass incursions of humanity do not tarnish the wildness of Tuckerman Ravine. In some ways, humanity augments its natural wildness by introducing a wildness of our own. This is not an easy concept to swallow—we tend to see nature and human culture as opposites. Cronon and Snyder suggest, however, that the fecund, animating, creative, and destructive forces that we call wildness are the matrix for all creation, humanity included. Such a concept of wilderness breaks down the divide between humans and nature—rocks, plants, animals, and *Homo sapiens* make up a single pattern, expressing a common, wild essence.

Aside from the dazzling spectacles on the slopes, part of what makes the Tuckerman culture feel wild is the party attitude of many of its users. Where else in the backcountry do you hear a crowd sending up cheers that could rival Fenway Park? Skiers have even been known to hike up to the ravine with beer kegs strapped to their packs. This style of wildness thrills at casting off conservative social mores, at living large and indulgently. It bears more than a passing resemblance to other rituals where the cultural order retreats, like Mardi Gras. Is this bacchanalian form of wildness really in keeping with that imagined by Cronon and Snyder? It's difficult to equate the wild of the backcountry slopes with the wild of a frat party. Perhaps the two concepts are irreconcilable. Yet both types of wildness at Tucks—whether in the form of extreme skiing or extreme revelry —find room to coexist within an evolving outdoor ritual.

America's understanding of wilderness is largely a history of how we have valued and symbolized wild places but, in the recent evolution of extreme sports and high adventures, it serves increasingly as a foil for seeing ourselves. We pit ourselves against the elements not so much to see them, but to test our own mettle. This ritual of self-imposed challenge uses danger as a tool, as a way of guaranteeing that the challenge is real. Without danger, we would have nothing to lose, and therefore nothing to gain.

It's true that everyone arrives at Tucks with a different set of motivations, which could be grouped broadly as serious or playful. For the serious faction of Tucks skiers, the ravine is their chance to test their judgment and skill. As weather and snow conditions shift rapidly, they continually reassess whether runs are feasible. They might pull out their snow saws and shovels to test the strength of a snow column. They scout their runs with care, and when they make a flashy run, you can be certain that they've analyzed the safest route. The serious skiers have seen enough accidents to hold a healthy respect for the mountain. They pick their challenges carefully and do not take stupid risks.

The other, perhaps larger, faction of skiers acts more or less oblivious to the ravine's dangers and are there to play. Generally, they are the ones you notice bouncing and flailing their way down the face. They take unusual risks at Tucks in part because they know they can be rescued. They accept the challenge on different terms: not to test their abilities but to test their limits. When judged through the criterion of safety, these skiers' playfulness is reckless at best. But perhaps it is this very quality of being ill-prepared that lends power to this ritual.

Several summers ago, while I was serving as a caretaker at Crag Camp for the Randolph Mountain Club on the northern ridge of Mount Adams, a group of hikers failed to return from a day hike up

Mount Washington. The blue skies of morning had vanished with that classic lack of warning. Soon after, thick fog and chill drizzle inundated the peaks. Disoriented, the hikers followed the wrong set of cairns over the headwall of King Ravine, a wild and boulder-strewn wilderness several thousand feet below Crag Camp. Realizing their mistake as the sun set, they chose to spend the night in the ravine in the drenching rain, with neither sleeping gear nor shelter, rather than attempt to recover their path. I, meanwhile, spent most of the night searching adjacent trails for them and initiating preliminary search-and-rescue protocol. They returned to Crag Camp the next morning, soaked to the bone and decidedly hypothermic. From the perspective of a caretaker and medical first-responder, I was tempted to upbraid them for their mistake. Yet they hiked out alive, with an indelible impression of the mountain's wildness. For all their misadventure, they received a keener taste of the danger and challenge than most hikers.

Later that summer, I attempted a similar day hike. I left the floor of King Ravine and began bushwhacking up its steep slope toward Crag Camp a thousand feet above. On a lark, I was hoping to find the remnants of a disused hiking trail printed in some ancient AMC topographic map. I never did find that trail, but I did discover a secluded gully with a pretty waterfall. Then the rain arrived. I almost took a long fall while scrabbling up a slick arête, and next I found myself in the lower bands of krummholz where the ground disappeared beneath a tangle of tree limbs. I made my way from limb to limb up the slope, feet slipping on the wet bark and hands grasping at boughs for support. As I ascended, the trees grew dense and murky with shadows. No longer able to slip between them, I proceeded on hands and knees, tunneling through a primeval forest of stunted spruce. After a full afternoon in the bush, I finally intersected a trail on the ridge. My knees were thoroughly bruised, my rain gear soaked and shredded, my hair a mess of needles, and my hands bleeding, gummy with tree resin, and caked in soil. I crawled out of the krummholz onto the trail like some creature emerging from a primordial womb. The short hike back to the cabin had never felt so easy by comparison. As I stepped inside Crag Camp, fellow hikers taking shelter from the storm shot me looks of "What the hell happened to you?" But all I could do was smile back. I had encountered true wilderness on the mountain and felt happy and alive.

Perhaps these days we seek danger in wilderness precisely because we have come so far in adapting to, and thereby domesticating, its challenges. We no longer beat ourselves up in the backcountry unless we are wholly unprepared. When our detailed topographic maps, high-tech fabrics, and ample food supplies offer easy solutions to the problems of navigation, comfort, and sustenance, it's difficult to experience the sensations of true trepidation and awe that earlier Americans sometimes felt. The antidote to this taming of wilderness lies in tackling the big challenges—big mountains, big cliffs, big waves, big treks, big depths, big heights, big exposure. To venture into wilderness is no longer enough; now we throw ourselves into it, sometimes with skill, sometimes with abandon. If so, American wilderness philosophy has come full circle. At first, our ancestors feared the dangerous wilderness and extolled civilization. Later we began to fear civilization and admire wilderness. Now, having driven much of the danger out of both society and the wilderness experience, we fear domestication, and we head off in search of danger. Danger becomes a tool for removing our acquired mental constructs; demanding our full attention, it allows us to devote our undivided attention to our immediate experience, the essence of the present moment, and perhaps the essence of our own being. Paradoxically, it is at crowded places like Tuckerman Ravine that experts and idiots alike find a suitable degree of danger to reveal their inner wildness.

It's instructive that the most heralded ritual each spring at Tucks is the modern incarnation of a classic race called the Inferno, a modern pentathlon that's big in every sense. Racers run, kayak or canoe, bike, hike to the summit of Washington, and finally ski Tuckerman Ravine. In its original form during the 1930s, the Inferno was solely a grand slalom race from the summit of Washington to its base. Of all the events in Mount Washington's storied history, perhaps none is more famous than the race of 1939, when a young Austrian contender named Toni Matt misjudged the location of his run and schussed the headwall, beelining it to the bottom at death-defying speeds of over 80 miles per hour and finishing in 6 minutes and 29.2 seconds, less than half the previous record. The legend of Toni Matt has become the proverbial sword in the stone for subsequent generations of headwall skiers who vie to rival his courage or stupidity. Although few athletes today attempt to schuss the headwall like Toni Matt, or boast the endurance to compete in all five events, the ritual of challenge hangs like a veil over the ravine.

* * *

On the slope, a team of medics and volunteers sets to work on my friend. One volunteer stabilizes the leg while I support his torso. A USFS medic slips a splint around the injury and fastens it in place, providing immense relief to his pain. We measure his vital signs, offer him a fistful of Advil, and make preparations for the two-hour evacuation to the valley. At this moment, I'm wholly relieved that Tucks is not your classic wilderness area. I'll happily trade skiing isolated, pristine peaks for an uncomplicated and life-saving rescue. I think my buddy would agree.

As the sun sets behind the rim of the cirque and the snow begins to harden, I boot to the top of the Chute to retrieve my friend's skis. Seven hundred feet up, I gingerly kick my way out into the middle of the run, and pull the blades from their sheaths of frozen snow. The sky is taking on hues of purple and the sun bathes the summit of Washington in yellows and golds. Looking over my shoulder into the darkening abyss below, I get a whiff of one reason we love the danger and the challenge. It is wildly beautiful.

Wilderness isn't simply a place on the map, but also our attitude toward that place. We can find it equally by refusing to domesticate the backcountry and by refusing to domesticate ourselves in the backcountry, by choosing the routes that challenge our skills and test our limits. Hopefully, we approach its dangers as calculated risk while retaining competence and sound judgment. But it is that wild edge of adventure, fraught with danger, that best reveals to us modern Americans the truth of wilderness. In that edge is an alchemy that brings us our senses and seals our ritual with danger's beautiful kiss.

NOTES

1 The essay appears in an anthology Cronon edited, *Uncommon Ground: Toward Reinventing Nature* (New York: W. W. Norton & Co., 1995).

2 Roderick Nash quotes Snyder in *Wilderness and the American Mind*.

6

The Northeast's True Hundred-Mile Wilderness?

* * *

RICK OUIMET

2009, Runner-up

 When it comes to wilderness, does federal designation matter? My wife and I first entertained this question after learning that the U.S. Congress had added the Wild River drainage to the White Mountain National Forest's five wilderness areas. Unfurling and connecting our trail-worn New Hampshire maps on the floor of our one-bedroom Manhattan apartment, a powerful possibility grabbed hold of our imagination: Could we fashion a one-hundred-mile hike, on established trails whenever possible, through the Whites' official wildernesses? If so, how would it compare to a trek on Maine's famed but not officially designated Hundred-Mile Wilderness, at the same time of the year and in a comparable amount of time? Not only did we have our next journey, but also a compelling face-off for the Northeast's true wilderness experience.

Wilderness is as hard to define, though, as it is to find. What is the goal? No people? No roads? No human intervention? Appropriately, we turned to the Guy and Laura Waterman vision of wilderness. That is, could we find solitude in a beloved region that attracts millions of annual visitors? Could we find inaccessibility with major state and national highways truncating these six wilderness areas? Could we find difficulty amid painstakingly maintained stone steps and trail ladders? Could we find the spirit of wildness in the face of manipulation?

Armed with these questions, we walked into the wild.

Day One
Caribou-Speckled Mountain Wilderness
Trail Mile 10

Almost on cue, it starts raining. I'm not going to just roll over. If I want this, I'm going to have to fight for it. It may have been sunny in Bethel, Maine, thirty minutes earlier, but as we crawl out of the car to begin our assault of White Mountain wilderness, a tempest is brewing. The wilderness is asserting itself, portending a difficult week ahead.

The weather is just the beginning. This is not Pinkham or even Kinsman Notch. Forget the quaint New England lodge or the spacious parking lot with privies. Just finding the Miles Notch Trailhead is a coup. The poor fellow from the bed-and-breakfast who agreed to drive us mutters, "Thank God this is a rental," each time the muffler meets rock. Finally spotting the tiny White Mountain National Forest placard indicating that this is indeed the trailhead for the westernmost wilderness area in the Whites, we find ourselves, oddly, at the brink of a four-acre clear-cut.

Pack covers secured, we head south through the minefield, less mindful of our lofty goal than of negotiating our way through stumps, debris, and mud in order to locate the trail. We eventually cross what we believe is Miles Brook, but as we're surrounded by softwood slash, we can only hope we're in the right place. A tense ten minutes of uncertain navigation brings a double "Eureka!" Not only have we found the trail and a healthy hardwood forest, but we've found the perfect place to begin a wilderness trail. Without a doubt, the unnerving location of the trailhead and its rough first half-mile will suppress future hiker traffic. And the active logging, the antithesis of wilderness, provides the perfect juxtaposition.

Just north of Miles Notch, a hand-chiseled wooden sign announces our entrance into the Caribou-Speckled Wilderness. Before we can snap the requisite picture at this symbolic cartographical boundary, lightning flashes overhead. With no AMC hut or shelter to run to, we huddle beneath a cluster of striped maples, sitting on our packs, shivering underneath our rain jackets, hugging our knees to keep our legs dry. The pelting rain drowns out all other sound. We've backpacked together long enough to read each other's thoughts: *What are we doing out here? Are you feeling as lonely as I am? Do you want to walk back to town before dark? To say we feel overmatched by nature is an understatement. But isn't that the point? Haven't we just found the wilderness we seek?*

Then magic. The rain slackens. Heading east on the Red Rock Trail, we crest a hemlock ridge with the perfect treadway. Squishy underfoot, the twisty path is narrow, barely as wide as the human frame, and seems, judging by the moose and bobcat scat, frequented almost exclusively by the four-legged variety. Its Vibram virginity allows the forest floor to rise with annual decomposition. The trail is on the brink of natural reclamation, yet it sees just enough foot traffic—perhaps a dozen people a week—to maintain viability. Equilibrium prevails.

Ambling along this euphoric ridge, occasionally dipping into birch cols with ferns reaching our waists, I am stunned that in a decade of crisscrossing the Whites we've never visited this Eden. Peering into the fog on the highest peak in the range, I have the reason. At 2,900 feet, Speckled Mountain lacks the increasing grandeur of the parallel ranges to the west—the Baldfaces at 3,600 feet, the Carters at 4,800 feet, the Presidentials at 6,200 feet. If the Carters are Washington's neglected younger brothers, then Speckled-Caribou has to be the forgotten pet hamster. The sense of solitude is indeed inversely proportional to the drop in elevation and distance east from Washington. It's also in between worlds. We're in Maine, oxymoronic for those who equate the Whites with New

Hampshire. With too many exciting alternatives, coming to the Caribou region demands a deliberate choice. Your hiking sensibilities have to have evolved enough to ignore the hedonistic impulse to revisit the Franconia Ridge.

Day Two
Wild River Wilderness
Trail Mile 22

At our stealth campsite near the infant Bickford Brook, we rise with first warbling of an ovenbird. Two major crossings loom 1,500 feet below. While fording the Cold River tests our traditional wilderness skills, traversing paved Maine 113 jeopardizes our wilderness vision and day-old solitude.

We ford for two reasons. Although we have no choice in crossing four roads and a cog railway to link these wilderness areas, we do control whether we use bridges. As fording is the more primordial, more difficult option, it's a no-brainer. Second, using a bridge in this instance would require significant road walking. As contact with asphalt has to be kept to fleeting seconds, we must bushwhack on this wilderness "trail" several times.

After drying our feet and re-lacing our boots, we sprint across Maine 113 before rush hour, neither seeing nor hearing a car, then bushwhack along the north side of Basin Pond to avoid the campground and boat launch on the far shore. The mist rising off the pond feeds the illusion of human-free nature.

Heading perpendicularly for the Baldface Range on the Basin Trail, the feeling of solitude faces a double threat: we are now not only in New Hampshire, we're also one range closer to Washington. But we may be safer than we realize. Switchbacking up to Rim Junction, a low pass on the ridge, we have adopted an unfamiliar, western hiking style akin to that of the John Muir Trail in California's Sierra Nevada, which treads pass to pass, rarely summiting peaks, never running ridges. With grand views, its high passes feel like summits. Eastern backpackers, by contrast, clamor for the ridge trails—Appalachian, Franconia, Meader—out of vista necessity. Briefly cresting wooded ridges only to plunge into their vast, featureless inter-regions does little for most Northeastern hikers. At least initially.

The dilapidated Blue Brook shelter and a few empty tent platforms along Spruce Brook compromise the palpably wild character of this infantile wilderness area, but we luck out and see no people, raising interesting questions: What if it were Saturday? What if it weren't raining yesterday in Caribou? Is this solitude irregular?

Day Three
Great Gulf Wilderness
Trail Mile 36

Animal encounters are conventional wilderness barometers. Ask any Northeastern enthusiast to define wildness, and she'll mention loons and moose; we saw both the previous week in Maine, trumped only by the fisher near Gulf Hagas.

But wild behavior from less charismatic creatures is equally telling. Near No Ketchum Pond, a mother grouse, hissing loudly, charges within inches of us, retreating to her chicks after we retreat in fear. We've experienced such grouse behavior before only in Quebec's remote Chic-Chocs. We give this feisty anomaly a wide berth.

Crash! Moments later, a bruin bushwhacks onto the trail and dashes away from us. Our first White Mountain bear-sighting ever! Its healthy flight instinct distinguishes this bear from its people-acclimated brethren we've met in Yosemite and Shenandoah.

At Perkins Notch, we pause at the lightly trodden Rainbow Trail, which climbs to Carter Dome. We reluctantly spurn this inviting path, abiding by another self-imposed rule: no 4000-footers on this trek. While this approach may be desolate, 4832-foot Carter Dome is bagged frequently from other directions. While peakbagging disperses hikers into unfamiliar corners of the range, it renders such summits increasingly familiar. Sit atop even the most isolated high peak—Owl's Head or Cabot—for a few summer hours, and you'll enjoy spirited conversations.

We enter boulder-strewn Carter Notch with the stealth of deer hunters. Lethal to our mission, it houses an AMC hut (even if one of the least visited). As luck has it, our midday, midweek arrival leaves the camp deserted. Even the caretaker is out re-supplying. We sign the log, "In Search of Wilderness—One Hundred Miles from Caribou to Sandwich," succumbing to the odd urge to leave evidence of our quest for solitude.

Leaving the notch, we reluctantly walk a brief section of the magnetic Appalachian Trail. Even though we are proud former Georgia-to-Mainers, we consider its wide, beaten treadway the antithesis of our new "reclaimed" paradigm. Our sacrilegious act proves a jinx, for our fifty-four hour people-free streak ends on a bog-bridge next to Carter Pond. An initial urge to resent this solitary hiker vanishes when we pass four guys wading in the Nineteen-Mile Brook shortly afterward.

Time to reflect. The solitude we've crafted thus far in this bustling range is encouraging. During the previous week, a hike from Monson to Abol Bridge in Maine's Hundred-Mile Wilderness yielded over a hundred people, including eight large groups. While that person-per-mile average is far better than typical backpacking trips in the Whites, we're far below that number this week. To be fair, Maine's trail never crossed a paved road, but it did intersect four improved logging roads, all providing day-hiker access, and an active railway (the midnight train whistle at Wilson Stream Lean-To bearing proof). An even more jarring moment occurred at pristine Jo-Mary Lake, where the sound of loons one minute was replaced by a hydroplane the next.

Back to New Hampshire. If we faced piranha yesterday at Route 113, we face crocodiles at Route 16 today. After waiting for a lull in the incessant traffic, we leap into the breach like a couple of wildebeests, feet hitting pavement fewer than eight times. The ensuing half-mile bushwhack takes nearly two hours due to thick underbrush and intense fords of the Peabody's twin forks. Fortuitously, this delays our arrival at the Great Gulf Trail until early evening, thinning the day-hiking crowd. We pass only four more hikers, but do nearly trip over several tents. For a potentially devastating day, seeing only nine Homo sapiens is a victory.

Day Four
Dry River Wilderness
Trail Mile 51

The crux awaits. Mount Washington's urban summit cone separates the Great Gulf and the Dry River (two of the Northeast's finest wildernesses) more effectively than Scylla and Charybdis. To preserve the continuity of this backpack, we have no choice but to navigate through and hope for survival. The wilderness anathemas are abundant: radio towers, cars, parking lots, a food court (with its admittedly tantalizing chili), a cog railway, and throngs of people. Expecting to have Washington to ourselves in any month (let alone August) is as naïve as expecting solitude in Central Park.

To give ourselves a fighting chance, we employ the Waterman philosophy. As Guy and Laura illustrate in Wilderness Ethics, ninety percent of the hiking crowd gravitates toward one or two trails up the popular peaks (in this case, the Tuckerman Ravine Trail and Ammonoosuc Ravine Trail, both half the mileage and requiring 1,000 feet less of elevation gain than our Great Gulf ascent and Dry River descent), while almost no one uses the first three hours of reliably people-free daylight. Thus, if you choose the right trail and leave early, even the most visited peak can beget solitude.

The headwall trail proves a time-swallowing adversary, however. It is a linear 1,600-foot scramble in under a mile, literally straddling a waterfall for short stretches. It slows us to a rock climber's pace;

we left at sunrise to beat the first cog, but its whistle and noxious coal plume hovering above Lake Spaulding herald our defeat. Yet we're too absorbed in this 5.3-level climb to mind. William Hart, who also built the insanely wonderful Six Husbands Trail, understood the nexus between difficulty and wildness. At an hour when hundreds of people switchback up Tuckerman, we encounter no one. Pulling ourselves up onto Bigelow Lawn is akin to lifting ourselves up onto the Grand Traverse in the Shawangunks.

Our unconventional assault of the Northeast's most celebrated peak requires that we forgo the chili and run a mile down the Gulfside Trail toward Jefferson (eleven backpackers passed), then contour south beneath the summit on the Westside. Although we can relax on this mostly ignored trail, the expansive above-treeline view —replete with a grand hotel, ski resort, and pastoral Lancaster countryside force us to contend with a sobering reality: nearly all Northeastern panoramas reveal evidence of humans, even if bucolic. Mount Bond in the middle of the Whites comes closest to the primeval vistas associated with Mount Kaweah in the Sierra Nevada or Gannett Peak in the Wind River Range, but its access trails are human highways. If you want to feel completely alone, forget treeline.

For the final leg of the Washington challenge, we opt for the longer Davis and Camel Trails as opposed to the shorter but congested Crawford Path. Heads down as if searching for Labrador tea or some equally obscure alpine flower, we pretend we can't see the scores of people milling around Lakes of the Clouds or those climbing the intervening quarter mile of talus. It begs the question of who counts—people passed or people seen. We opt for the former. Counting the latter would squash our Maine total in an hour.

Gazing over the Dry River Valley at the Oakes Gulf headwall, it's indisputable that this 6200-feet behemoth, despite inherent problems, spawns wilderness. Its drainages are vast, creating the anonymous realms fundamental to solitude. Miles of nondescript spruce and birch stand below us.

Four miles down, now lost in the chasm we had just peered over, we've become part of the forest, of the inter-peak region. Our only rivals are an intrepid father-daughter tandem heading for Washington.

At our Dry River Wilderness campsite, we relive this exciting day, relishing our survival. Like hares scampering from burrow to burrow under an eagle's aerie, we necessarily tempted fate before plunging back into the forested abyss.

Day Five
Pemigewasset Wilderness
Trail Mile 70

Washington was a thrilling midpoint, offering the week's peak elevation, difficulty, and crowds. Looking forward, another potential bookend of solitude awaits.

Darting across yet another highway, a mid-hike crisis seeps in. Are we not heavily contriving this sense of wilderness, mirroring the problematic nature of prescribed wilderness areas themselves? Just as deeming nature "wilderness" is a conspicuously human act, we conspicuously avoid summits and pretend that people seen (but not passed) do not exist. Now we're heading for a sliver of the most visited wilderness area in the Whites, the Pemigewasset. Why? Bounded by fifteen 4,000-footers, this beloved area is, in Roderick Nash's famous words, "in danger of being loved to death." It even has its own visitor center.

Heavily wooded Owl's Head, in the middle of the Pemigewasset, is the appropriate destination, but its 4,023-foot elevation ensures more daily traffic than a week on Speckled. Plus, its approaches are heavily traveled. So, for the first time on this trek, we compromise, choosing not to traverse the breadth of a wilderness area, instead grazing the Pemigewasset's remote southeastern corner. Before this contrived isolation, we contend with a contrived three-mile bushwhack sandwiched between Route 302 and the Conway Scenic Railway.

As we climb under old-growth spruce to windswept Nancy Pond, however, we repeat the mantra of this hike: Why haven't we been here yet? With the Southern Presidentials a mere stone's throw away, the question is rhetorical. The mature trees mirror our maturing hiking psyche.

A ledge at Norcross Pond furthers our wonderment, providing an unexpected view of the Bonds' eastern slopes. While hundreds feast on the western side of this range each summer day from Franconia Ridge, only dozens know this underbelly (only four others so far today). The carpeted descent toward Stillwater Junction, softened further by the late afternoon's filtered sunlight, belies its logging past.

To continue our streak of sleeping within the actual wildernesses, we pitch our tent in a dry gully a few hundred feet from imposing Carrigain Notch, the borderland. The sun sets two hours earlier tonight, discomfortingly comforting.

Day Six
Sandwich Range Wilderness
Trail Mile 86

It's a sloppy morning. After rolling up a tent saturated from three overnight thunderstorms, we trudge along the boggy Sawyer River Trail, often shin-deep in mud. Fording the burly, bridgeless Swift is an ablution.

We feel like Survivor Man at the Kancamagus Highway, the last paved obstacle of the journey. Maybe we are too wet, or perhaps we've successfully found wilderness and are hence intrigued by this asphalt anomaly, but this time we actually linger, mesmerized by a loud eighteen-wheeled beast chugging toward Kancamagus Pass, water spewing from her tires. Part of us wants to be inside the cab, heading somewhere dry. We are tired and hungry. The metal bear seems as humbled by this wilderness as we do.

Twice losing our way on the Livermore Trail, we feel truly lonely for the first time since Miles Notch. Even in sunshine, this could be Walden. Or Anchorage Bus 142 on the Stampede Trail. Who would believe this was once a busy thoroughfare connecting Waterville with the Pemigewasset logging camps?

Topping nondescript Livermore Pass, my eyes blur from countless shades of green, sharpened by the dark fog. This overgrown trail limits the scope to a few square feet of forest, allowing us to see the proverbial forest for its mosses, lichens, and ferns amid ancient rockfall. The road to wilderness stops for botany and geology.

We could spend an entire week in this intoxicating piece of forest, but Mount Tripyramid's rugged South Slide, buffering the western edge of the Sandwich Range Wilderness, beckons. We yearn to hike the even more difficult North Slide, but doing so necessitates crossing two 4,000-footers. The rules of the game dictate our every move.

Paradise strikes again: the Kate Sleeper Trail. Her earthly sign, visible only when descending the slide and barely wider than the spruce trunk it hangs from, is so inconspicuous that the Wonalancet Club must hope you miss it. After an initial steep drop, Kate becomes pure boreal bliss, snaking along the finest of all the forgotten trails of this hike. We wend our way through sunlit balsam heaven, never having to break stride, but feeling compelled to tiptoe in this cathedral.

Kate's a guilty pleasure. We selfishly want her all to ourselves, knowing that "getting the secret out" undermines her sponginess and incomparable solitude. So why even write about it?

Clambering over a maze of uneven boulders around clandestine Flat Mountain Pond, we agree that on the Appalachian Trail this gem would enjoy rock-star status and have a dull, improved trail to boot. The only soul within miles (that we know of) is, not surprisingly, a peakbagger on Whiteface.

Sandwich Dome's 3,993-foot elevation means that two boreal chickadees are our only company. How different the mountain would feel were it seven feet taller. With wild views into the bowls of the Whites extending to Baldface, six days distant, Sandwich is a worthy Katahdin. We loiter.

The five-mile descent via Smart Brook (the most obscure route on this already lonely mountain) makes for a fitting end. Twisting our way atop brown carpet, stopping only to negotiate blowdowns and to admire mossy, car-sized boulders, we have found the Red Rock Trail's double, bookending the week. To enhance the symmetry, Smart abruptly dead-ends in a clear-cut, just minutes from Route 49, belying one hundred miles of nearly contiguous wilderness.

Making a beeline for Waterville Valley, we have little interest in debating whether we have found the authentic hundred-mile wilderness trail. Hot showers and food take precedence. Once satiated, however, we reconsider the question and answer *yes*.

It goes beyond the math (which the Whites won handily: 27 people passed compared to 112 in Maine). It transcends the complicated question, "Which is truly wilder?" and the problematically qualitative one, "Which feels wilder?" Ironically, it's the contriving, the heavily bemoaned "game" that gives the victory to the Whites and, more importantly, yields pragmatic implications for actually preserving wilderness. Just as most designated Northeast wildernesses attempt to restore old growth, this trail restores the imagination.

Ecosystem-minded opponents of federal wilderness areas rightfully criticize "freeze-framing" nature, and while such artificial places are perhaps imperfect vehicles, they do get us thinking about wilderness. For wilderness to exist in the mind, it needs nurturing. Challenging its very essence is a good start. To its detriment, Maine lacks such controversy.

Moreover, a true wilderness trail can never become a static destination for the masses. Maine's storied past proves self-effacing. It's too easy for the hiker; if he wants wilderness, he knows where to go, without having to think about where to go. He never creates a destination. Numbers skyrocket. Shelters rise.

Since New Hampshire lacks a celebrated wilderness trail, and since most of the wilderness areas don't make the greatest hits album, coming to Caribou, et al., involves self-sacrifice. In the few popular wildernesses, avoiding the hordes demands creativity. The heavy lifting is left to the individual.

A true wilderness trail is thus metaphorical, amid which the process of discovery trumps any actual route. Like wilderness itself, it is constantly in a state of becoming, each success inspiring other possibilities—such as the new goal already taking shape on our apartment floor, this one linking the Whites' wildest non-wilderness areas from Carr Mountain to Albany Notch. One preferred trail replaces another even before overuse becomes an issue. And once abandoned, by choice or necessity, a route reclaims itself, perhaps to be used again. This process guarantees dispersion, minimizing hardened campsites and orange-peel-littered summits.

Guy Waterman understood this game brilliantly, always seeking the next project that would take him to ever more remote corners of the Whites. He offers a story of constant movement, of process over destination. Like Guy, we must emulate true wilderness by constantly evolving, from traversing Franconia Ridge to peakbagging to exploring forgotten trails to climbing technical routes to becoming ephemeral visitors of nondescript backcountry. If we play the game right, evidence of our visit vanishes almost instantly. I therefore write about Kate, Livermore, and Red Rock with confidence. Those inclined toward our route have already evolved, and the few who come will not stay long.

William Wordsworth played the game too, understanding that wilderness resides in the imagination; he called a primeval experience on Wales's Mount Snowdon "the perfect image of a mighty mind." If we can dream up that perfect new route, constantly finding wilderness in familiar areas, then our beloved peaks and valleys just may feel, if not be, forever wild.

7

Hunting the Woolly Adelgid

* * *

DIANNE FALLON

2010, Winner

 I have been tramping in the woods near Mount Agamenticus in southern Maine for a couple of hours, looking for signs of a tiny aphid-like insect that kills hemlock trees, and I am starting to feel hungry and cold. I should have brought more snacks. I'm feeling a bit uncertain about the scientific aspect of the survey I have volunteered to do. I'm supposed to plot data on a sheet, following the compass points spelled out in the instructions—but I think I can figure it out: Start with the first hemlock tree, examine two branches of new foliage, walk twenty-five paces, find another tree, check it. Check the sheet for the next cardinal point, use the compass to orient myself, and walk another twenty-five paces in that direction. My goal is to check one hundred hemlock trees in this random but directed fashion.

I have come here today to survey my adopted tree stand for signs of the woolly adelgid because I love hemlocks, the way their lacy branches spread out and make the woods into a cathedral. In the winter, I love seeing the patches of packed-down snow beneath a hemlock's sheltering branches—evidence that deer are keeping themselves cozy and warm. And I love these woods, and the opportunity to experience them in a different way—to get out into the forest with my compass and follow the directions for the survey, wandering in terrain I might not otherwise explore. I like having a purpose to direct my wandering, to take me into patches of the forest where I might not go otherwise. I like feeling as if I am taking care of these trees.

The day is overcast, a little chilly, but not cold. This is strange weather for mid-December. On Thursday night came the freezing cold which caused an ice storm that snapped branches and toppled trees. On Friday, a blast of warm air melted the ice within hours. Today, colder air has blown in. We've been camping out at the house without power for five days, stoking the woodstove and flushing the toilet with water siphoned from standing pools into a trash barrel. On this Monday, ten days before Christmas, I have student portfolios to grade, errands to run, and a children's birthday party to organize. Coming to the woods today takes time away from these responsibilities, but I consider it time well spent, an antidote for this frenzied time of year.

Earlier, driving up Mountain Road, I navigated debris from the ice storm littering the road: pine needles, branches, and limbs pushed off to the sides. No lights or other signs of electricity in the homes set back on wooded lots. I passed two Central Maine Power trucks, their crews floating in buckets amid the power lines as they worked to restore order from the tangled mess created by the storm. I knew that I would have to be vigilant for hanging limbs in the treetops—widow-makers—that might snap and break. Was I crazy to be out here today? Maybe, but I felt confident that most branches weak enough to break had already done so.

As I drove past the Mount Agamenticus access road, I ignored the Road Closed sign and continued up Mountain Road as pavement gave way to dirt. This portion is officially closed December to April, but that doesn't mean the road is impassable, at least not until the first heavy snow. I drove to the high point where a cliff overlooks a ravine, and then down the steep hill toward Cedar Creek. I had to slow down and drive around a white pine that lay on one side of the road, blocking the opposite lane. After parking my car at the Cedar Creek trailhead, I set off, walking down the old tote road. My map shows that this old road leads to a pond, so I walked to the pond and then plunged into the woods from there, making that area the first block of my survey.

Although I live in southern coastal Maine, an area that feels more suburban than rural, today I am alone out here. This patch of forest feels as remote as any that I've walked in the North Woods or in New Hampshire's White Mountains. Maybe even more so, because when I hike in the Whites, I take trails. When I visit my tree stand, I wander.

My tree stand is part of the largest unfragmented coastal forest between Acadia National Park and the New Jersey Pine Barrens. The forest here has been preserved in small and large parcels by ten conservation groups working together, the Mount Agamenticus to the Sea Coalition—an effort that began over one hundred years ago, when the local water district began to buy up land to protect the water supplies for the towns of York and Kittery. This sprawling stretch of undeveloped land—about 30,000 acres—stretches from the backside of 691-foot Mount Agamenticus to slivers of marshland along the York River.

Like almost all land in New England, these 30,000 acres have been used and developed in many ways over the centuries: for farming, sheep grazing, lumber. During World War II, a radar tower —the first of its kind in the United States—was installed on the summit of Mount A and the forest cut to make room for barracks to house twenty-five soldiers of the 551st Signal Battalion. For ten years in the 1960s and 1970s, a ski area drew locals to the mountain each winter.

Today, telemark skiers trek up Mount A to turn on slopes that shrink a bit more each season as trees and brush take over. When the snow melts, hikers and casual visitors wander the summit's open meadow, bikers careen down the rocky trails, and the mountaintop can feel like a busy place, like the top of Mount Washington on a clear day. But even with the people there, the blue ocean shimmers to the east. To the west, the spine of Mount Washington rises above the Ossipee Hills, a spectacular sight any day but especially on a clear spring afternoon, when the sloping ridge of Washington remains covered in snow.

These woods below the slope of Mount A are the deepest and thickest area in this vast tract of protected land. A rambler can tramp for hours without seeing a house or road. Although the woods welcome their share of dog walkers and mountain bikers, especially on the weekends, most people, myself included, tend to overlook this wildness in their own backyard. It's only in recent years that I have taken to exploring this terrain. Somehow we have the idea that the woods are wild only if they are remote.

In the past, instead of looking for wildness in my own neighborhood, I sought it in more distant locales: in climbing 4,000-footers in New Hampshire, in bushwhacking in Arctic national parks, and while listening for lions on Mount Kenya. Only when my travels were curbed by family responsibilities did I begin to view the Agamenticus forest as an opportunity to experience the wild.

And these woods are wild. A massive beaver lodge rises from the middle of the boggy pond. Are the beavers still living there, or have they abandoned this lodge? I examine the branches littering the shore, trying to determine if beavers have been gnawing at them, since I know that beavers will live in an area until they have exhausted the food supply, and then move on. The surface of the pond is patchy white. Maybe the surface is frozen, but it's certainly not ice. It's quiet here. As quiet as my house without electricity.

I breathe in the stillness, hopeful that I might see something —a deer, an elusive bobcat?—but I have missed the prime wildlife-watching hours of early morning. I know that bobcats live here because I have seen their snowy tracks on nearby Chase Pond. Wild turkeys roost in the trees and strut about on old logging roads. Wetlands such as this pond and nearby vernal pools are breeding

So what about the adelgids?

grounds for wood frogs, blue-spotted salamanders, and the rare spotted and Blanding's turtles. Earlier in the fall, on another drive up Mountain Road with my young son and his friend, we passed a Turtle Crossing sign, and then, as if the sign had conjured the creature, we came upon a spotted turtle crossing the road.

After a few minutes of enjoying the pond, I backtrack a few steps and plunge into the forest to do my survey. The forest floor is littered with natural debris—small brooms of leaves, tangles of branches and, here and there, a large limb that would have killed whatever creature happened to be passing as it fell. Some trees will wither and die from the effects of the ice storm, especially the weaker trees that can't recover from the loss of a thick upper limb. But overall, the forest looks healthy, green. The forest will survive this natural catastrophe.

But will it survive the woolly adelgid? This tiny insect is a killer, gluing itself to the twigs of hemlock foliage where it then sucks the sap within the tree's green needles. Hemlock trees infested with woolly adelgids usually die within four to ten years. This deadly Asian pest, which first appeared in the Northwest in the 1920s, showed up in the eastern United States, in Virginia, in the 1950s. Since then, it has been creeping south and north, carried along by animals, birds, and the wind. The insect has ravaged the eastern hemlock forests in southern Appalachia, creating large swaths of grayish-green dying or dead hemlocks. Now, the woolly adelgid has reached southern Maine. On the other side of Mountain Road —less than a hundred yards from my tree stand—many hemlocks are marked with surveyor's tape so that researchers and conservation workers know where the pests have been spotted.

To try to save the eastern hemlock in Maine, the Maine Forest Service has mobilized an army of volunteers, staff, and other conversation professionals to detect the woolly adelgids. Entomologists don't believe that they can stop or eradicate the woolly beast; containment is the goal. If these stewards of the forest find an area where the adelgids have invaded, the Forest Service moves in to attack the insects with a tiny black beetle, *Laricobius nigrinus*, that eats woolly adelgids. Nobody knows if this effort will be successful. The cold might kill the beetles. The beetles might not reproduce. Releasing the beetles, which are native to the Northwest, might provoke unintended consequences. Entomologists have evaluated this possibility and believe that the beetles will not upset the balance of the local ecosystem, but they can't be certain.

Other ways of saving the hemlocks also might prove to be successful. The Asian hemlock is resistant to the adelgids and scientists are experimenting with hybridizing this tree with its cousin, the eastern hemlock. And hemlock forests have been devastated before, but recovered—although in the past, people, not natural pests, caused the devastation, as they looted the trees of their bark to extract the tannins once used in the tanning industry.

I want to be hopeful for these beautiful trees, but sometimes I feel discouraged by the constant trickle of news about threats to our forests. Elongate hemlock scale, from Japan, also damages hemlocks. Other species of trees also face dire threats. Asian longhorned beetles have infested the maple trees in central Massachusetts and are creeping north, especially on firewood. The emerald ash borer already has killed millions of ash trees, just a few years after it was first discovered in the United States in 2002.

Sometimes all of this bad news about invasive insects feels overwhelming, especially in considering the consequences. We've lost our elm trees and our American chestnuts. Can we imagine the forest without hemlocks? Or a New England fall without maple trees? A spring without the sap running?

Our forests need care. In providing the care, in being with the trees, I can deflect the blows from the onslaught of bad news about invasive pests, diseases, and other problems. Although visiting my tree stand has made me more aware of all the threats facing the forest, I didn't know about all of these challenges when I signed on to be part of the Forest Service brigade, to adopt a hemlock tree stand, and check it every year for adelgids. I had seen an item in the newspaper about the insects and decided I want to be part of caring for these trees.

This year, I visited my tree stand in the fall, but it was too early, too warm, to see evidence of them. The adelgids form a protective woolly coating as the weather gets colder—they look like tiny pieces of fuzzy cotton, about the size of a wood tick. The best time to examine hemlocks for the adelgids is winter and early spring because they are more visible then, encased in their woolly coats, and because the surveyor is less likely to contribute to spreading the adelgids. In the late spring, mobile larvae known as crawlers emerge from the woolly sacs and will drift on anything that brushes up against an invaded twig.

Today, after a couple of turns and checking of foliage, I land on the bank of Cedar Creek, dark and swollen from the rain. Downstream a few paces, a cluster of rocks creates a bridge, and I cross over to the other side. Hemlocks rise all around me, a primeval cathedral. A few white pines are mixed into the forest, but mostly I am surrounded by hemlocks. This is what I love about hemlocks—the shade created by a mature hemlock stand doesn't allow lower-story trees or bushes to flourish, so a hemlock forest is open and airy, devoid of heavy brush.

I work steadily, hiking my twenty-five paces, in more or less the prescribed direction, climbing up a moss-covered rocky outcropping, then plunging back down toward the stream. At one point I look up and notice the shaking crown of a white pine—shaking because something is climbing in the tree—something heavier than a squirrel. Could it be a porcupine? I try to get a look, but the treetop crowns are dense, dark. Still, I feel elated to be so close to a wild animal doing what it does every day.

The forest floor is damp, spotted with puddles of standing water, but not icy. The ice melted the day after the storm, and it's easy to make my way through the woods. Walk twenty-five paces, stop, survey branches on one side of the tree, then another. So far, I have not spotted anything that is definitely a woolly adelgid, though I find two branches with whitish spots that could be adelgids, or something else, like clumps of dried-up sap.

I remind myself to look up for signs of breaking branches. The forest floor is covered with branches and limbs, and some trees are down, but overall the damage is less than what I expected. Do hemlocks—healthy ones—resist the damage of an ice storm that might kill other trees? I wonder if their foliage, its laciness, protects them by spreading out the weight of the ice.

These hemlocks, it seems, will survive the battering of the ice storm, but may not withstand the slow bleed of this invasive pest. I suppose we're not so different from this tree. We can survive a crisis, get knocked down and still get back up again, but the slow bleed of resentment or stultification does more damage.

I climb up the slope from the creek, scrambling over moss-covered rocks that help to anchor these hemlocks. Hiking in these woods in December reminds me that there are pleasures to savor in all seasons. The emptiness, the quiet, the lack of bugs. The opaque whiteness of the pond. The sound of chickadees calling. These woods today offer as much opportunity for joy as reaching a summit on a brilliant summer afternoon.

I've sampled almost fifty trees. Although I've bagged a couple of twigs with whitish spots, I'm pretty sure that the adelgids have not invaded this side of the road—not yet. I'll need to stop soon, so I won't meet my goal of sampling a hundred trees today. But that's OK. I'll have a reason to come here again soon on another day, alone, to wander in this forest, to feel this wildness so close to my everyday life.

The ice storm adds to the pleasures of this December ramble. The storm broke branches and downed trees, creating gaps and light, opening up patches of forest to the sun—opportunities for new life. The broken limbs and uprooted trees will provide food to uncounted insects, fungi, and other organisms. As for me, the storm has caused a shift in perspective. Instead of looking mostly forward, I look up.

8

The Red Squirrel and the Second Law, or, What the Caretaker Saw

* * *

JONATHAN MINGLE

2010, Runner-up

> Here where we are life wells up as a strong . . . spring
> perpetually . . . piling water on water . . . with the dancing high
> lights upon it. But it flows away on all sides as into a marsh
> of its own making. It flows away into poverty into insanity into
> crime . . . Dark as it is that there are these sorrows and darker
> still that we can do so little to get rid of them . . . the darkest
> is that perhaps we ought not to want to get rid of them . . .
> What life . . . craves most is signs of life.
>
> FROM *THE NOTEBOOKS OF ROBERT FROST*

 My first job was picking up sticks for our neighbor, when I was eleven. He was an engineer, a friendly but obsessive *Always* guy waging constant war against the understory in his two acres of Virginia pine woods. Whether he feared the fire threat of debris accumulation, or disdained nutrient recycling in general, I don't know. He paid me a few dollars an hour to walk through his woods, pick up every stick I found and pile it in his yard, so I did. *OCD*

The Kurtzian jungle that was our woods made the property line quite obvious. Thorny vines and thistle, beech saplings and kudzu and poison ivy all craned and crept toward the shattered light piercing the canopy. Walking to the neighbor's property involved a jarring transition, as I skirted the photosynthetic riot ringing our backyard. The sight of it all from his back patio must have raised the guy's blood pressure. His woods were like the forest primeval as imagined by the risk management department: stately pines widely spaced, low branches all pruned away, a soft bed of fragrant pine needles blanketing the floor. You could drive a truck through parts of it. And yet, for all the spaciousness and apparent peace, his woods felt dark and oppressive to me, next to the jangle of our unkempt forest. Not a single fern poked up through the uniform duff. No mushrooms or moss-digested logs broke its surface. Even the squirrels seemed chastened, on notice.

The absurdity of my task was not lost on me, even at my tender age. It didn't take long to clear out the big branches. But I soon discovered a seemingly inexhaustible supply of offending smaller sticks, half-submerged in the sea of needles. The longer I patrolled, more and more twigs registered in my field of vision. I began to feel like a lone diver harvesting grains of sand on the ocean floor. And, after the first hour or so of each session, my back got really sore.

All in all, it was an unappetizing foretaste of the working world —of its latent obsession with Cartesian order, of its unapologetic logic of suppression (or denial) of nature's insistent forces. My role as a pawn in a larger, little-explained war seemed vaguely troubling. All the more so when I found out later that the absence of undergrowth was partly due to his spraying it with some kind of Roundup-strength weed-killing cocktail. But at the time I had more pressing concerns, namely the purchase of a 1989 complete set of Topps Major League Baseball cards—enabled by my modest earnings. *another one*

Many years later I got a job as a hut caretaker with the Appalachian Mountain Club. I arrived for my first night in October, carrying a nasty head cold. Coming straight from a friend's wedding, on little sleep, I hiked up the Nineteen-Mile Brook Trail in blowing rain, and burst into the hut a sodden, hacking mess. That first week in Carter Notch proved to be representative of the season ahead of me: raw, wet weather, winds that whistled and wailed through the narrow cleft in the mountains. Built in 1914, the simple stone hut squats a few hundred yards from the shore of two crystalline lakes. Direct light is fleeting: the sun rises late over Carter Dome's shoulder, and sets early behind the cheek-by-jowl cliffs of Wildcat. On certain blustery December twilights, as the gusts rattle the door, the place feels like an Antarctic outpost, worthy of Shackleton.

Once my cold abated, caretaking thoroughly agreed with me. A softly padding fox did circuits in the mornings around the hut and the bunkhouses. I'd go out around dawn to check the snow stake and glance at the sky, and often see its fresh tracks stamped in the snow like an invitation. After I called in the weather on the radio, I'd go sweep out the bunkhouses and the bathrooms. The fox would sometimes precede me on my rounds, a hundred paces ahead. It would pause and look back at me over its graying haunches, intensely alert, curious, and (at the risk of some anthropomorphizing) maybe even bemused. In the evenings I emptied my sprung mousetraps in the snow next to the hut, by the morning the offerings would be gone, biochemically transmuted into pure fox motion.

Mornings and evenings I worked, and was on call, but the middle of the day I usually had to myself. After filling the water jugs from the lake (at night a thick new skin of ice would form, and I'd have to ax a new hole every morning), I would hike up to Carter Dome, walking as far along the Carter-Moriah Trail as my fancy would take me. Or I'd bushwhack down the valleys, ducking into the birch glades around Nineteen Mile Brook, or following the banks of the ice-cold Wildcat River south.

My destination-free rambles brought priceless surprises. One day I found a popular moose wallow in a thick tangle of snags half a mile south of the hut. I'd sometimes wander down there after lunch, and a couple times encountered two enormous moose enjoying their bachelorhood together, lazily browsing saplings, hulking and exhaling in the silence of a late afternoon. I'd get as close as I dared, until they'd tense up, swivel their huge racks and size me up, nostrils steaming. We'd stare at each other for five minutes or more, until one of us broke the spell and wandered back to our world apart, awkwardly crashing through the underbrush.

On one off day, while hiking across the valley, I sat contentedly in a clearing, watching high clouds scudding east. A finch alighted on a rock twenty feet away. It cocked its head and hopped about, as finches will do. I enjoyed its little show as I munched my sandwich. Then a blur from the firs smeared across my field of vision, ending in a cartoon puff of feathers and blood, from which a fisher cat emerged, clamping the finch in its jaws. Before I could process it all, it slunk back into the trees to enjoy its hard-earned lunch.

Such were my days. Gray jays would nearly land on my head as I ate peanuts on some granite perch. Raucous crows wheeled about the cliffs and swooped and jeered at me as I skated around the lake. Back in the hut, my dripping, grinning guests would pull off their wool hats upon arrival, revealing coifs worthy of Maurice Sendak's Wild Things as they huddled gratefully around the woodstove. "You get to live here?" they'd ask, incredulous.

The wildness of the Notch was less a full-throated Darwinian scream than a low and steady hum—punctuated by the occasional percussive encounter with some nonhuman Other, bottoming out in mutual mystery. With each passing day I lapsed further into a sweet, muted embrace of the unexpected.

It was the first job that really made sense to me.

Soon I had moved on to other mountains, other jobs. Good things, we're told, aren't meant to last.

This nostrum, it turns out, is really just a rough paraphrase of the second law of thermodynamics, which states that, in an isolated system, entropy tends to increase with time. Entropy is often described as a measure of how much molecular disorder there is in a system—spilling a glass of milk across the floor, or letting an ice cube melt on the table, for example, both entail an increase in entropy. It takes energy to return that milk or water to their original states, and in the process some energy must inevitably be lost as heat to the wider world.

As time progresses and entropy increases, the second law tells us, the energy concentrated in suns, caretakers, and gray jays must undergo irreversible dispersal. Hot flows to cold, the hut plumbing breaks, and time's arrow shoots implacably forward, as the system seeks some kind of irrevocable equilibrium.

Every new baby fox born in the Notch—and the evolutionary parade of life on earth in general—would seem to refute this grim dictum. After all, a fresh fox represents an improbable increase in order, a complex concentration of cells storing information and energy and matter, arrayed in elegant, furry, focused form. But, the second law mavens remind us, the birth of this fox amounts to a merely local decrease in entropy, which must be compensated by an even greater increase in the entropy of the surrounding environment. And Carter Notch, despite its remote feel, is not an isolated system. As the eminent biochemist Albert Lehninger explained in his 1982 textbook, Principles of Biochemistry, "living organisms preserve their internal order by taking from their surroundings free energy, in the form of nutrients or sunlight, and returning to their surroundings an equal amount of energy as heat and entropy."

Disorder is thus offloaded to the world at large. Or, to cite another paraphrase of the second law, there's no such thing as a free lunch. The new fox will digest the new caretaker's gift of new mice, yes, and this will fuel her roaming and hunting and curious glances. But as energy moves up the trophic ladder, only about 10 percent of each meal builds and fuels her cells; the rest, as with an incandescent bulb, is given off as waste heat, never to be recaptured.

Eventually, the fox, too, will be dispersed. For obvious reasons, the second law is cited by some as cause for despair. After all, it seems to augur an increasingly cold, dark, quiet universe, as the energy available for sustaining life ebbs and spills ever outward, as the concentration of information required for organizing life becomes impossible. As one scientist colorfully sums up the situation: "You can't win, you can't break even, you can't even drop out of the game."

And yet the denizens of the Notch gamely fight on. Is this what we mean by "wildness," this recalcitrance, this defiance of tough odds, dimly intuited?

For most of our history as a species, the "wild" alluded to a state of madness, a place of exile, bereft of method or comfort. To the casual observer still, the natural world (as we misleadingly qualify it, forgetting there's no other kind) can seem like an engine of disorder and chaos. Things grow and teem willy-nilly, devouring each other, grasping blindly, thoughtlessly, for fuel, space, and light. Unseen forces surge through stems and tides, driving countless organisms through the paces of an unchoreographed dance, both vast and minute. In the wild, after all, don't hunger and fear rule nakedly, *randomly* even?

We generally like to define nature in opposition to the realm of human artifice. Historically, we used "wild" to denote a zone beyond the frontier outpost walls, where that supposedly most human of attributes—rationality—is entirely absent. A zone that occasions awe and longing and fear, often mingled together, but always a place where we decidedly do not belong.

The wild is still that place in our imagination where anything goes, where young Max is free to indulge his Rumpus-ing urges. The Wild West was wild precisely insofar as it was lawless. A cursory glance at how we use the word today helps further trace its hard-to-shake psychic outlines. A "wild man" is uncontrollable, unpredictable, heedless of society's contrivances and constraints. A "wild pitch" is a focused effort gone astray. A "wild accusation"? Ungrounded in truth, reason, or fact. Hysterical. Despite some latter-day rehabilitation, and its more recent overtones of the sub-lime (thanks to the Romantic poets and the conservation move-ment of the twentieth century), "wild" remains a word with a dodgy pedigree, and often pejorative deployments. It can still leave that metallic taste of fear in the mouth.

On this conventional reading—a caricature perhaps, but one that still compels us—the engineer's woods might represent a Sis-yphean attempt to stave off chaos, embodied by the "wild," unruly process of forest succession. Whereas the daily tableaux of Carter Notch are a veritable hymn to humming, thrumming entropy, crea-tures scattering their energies amid a scrum of aimless, elemental forces.

But this superficial view, of which we're all at times guilty, makes a critical mistake. It conflates the "wild" with disorder and disarray.

In fact, the opposite is true. Grooming the grounds, suppress-ing life in those Virginia woods, was actually a rearguard action *on behalf of* entropy. What I witnessed every day in and around the Notch—the wary, browsing moose, the opportunistic fox, a thou-sand small acts of scavenge and savvy—was another chapter in an unfolding, many-faced stand *against* the ravages of time's arrow.

A year later, I was pulled back into the White Mountain fold, and found myself working in another hut, overlooking Zealand Falls. It didn't take long to settle into the familiar rhythms of the late-fall caretaking season. One night, as I enacted the pre-bed ritual —turning off lights, checking pilot lights, locking the rat-proof storage, filling my water bottle—I heard the distinctive pitter-patter of small mammalian feet on brushed aluminum.

A quick headlamp search located the source: a red squirrel, tensed and frozen mid-raid atop the stove hood. I shooed him and he scurried back up the vent, squeezing through the gap in the roof back into the cool night.

Things soon escalated from there. The red squirrel grew increas-ingly brazen, launching scavenging sorties across my carefully disinfected counters while I sat a few yards away reading by the woodstove. A couple of stray oats and a missed lump of brown sugar was all it took to tempt him down. At night, after I'd retire to the crew room, I'd sometimes hear him descend the stove vent, like a diabolical rodent version of St. Nick, to make his calorie-seeking circuit. I would race downstairs and swing a broom or a cutting board, and he would bound, without panic, to the safety of his stove-hood Switzerland. There he would often pause to vent at me with high-pitched chatter, before disappearing up the vent.

Though I knew it was just my frustration at work (keeping the kitchen clean is a top caretaker priority), I detected a scornful note in his vocalizations. I thought I knew what he was saying: "Sure, go ahead, yell, throw things, whatever. I will be here long after you're gone, my friend. You're the tourist, not me." The fact that he was right only infuriated me more. Some days, as I sat in the sun on the front porch, he would come up within a couple yards, then stop and screech at me with impunity, probably elaborating on his earlier point. Then, seized by some dark impulse, he would bound down the rocks out of sight.

I thought about packing up a Havahart trap on my next stint. On evening radio call, I began to inquire about borrowing a BB gun from a fellow caretaker. Had he been listening in, my old neighbor the engineer would have nodded in approval.

The red squirrel is an industrious planner for the winter. It picks mushrooms and places them in the crooks of trees to dry. It tears open spruce cones by the thousands, and caches their seeds in trees or burrows. Its midden is a telltale pile of cone debris, testifying to the fact that the squirrel is not a slacker, or a rank opportunist. But its spatial memory is less than perfect; the squirrel is prone to losing track of some caches, amid the deep snow and exigencies of a New Hampshire winter. Like any of us, his trophic demands call for insurance, a caloric buffer.

One afternoon I returned from a hike up Zeacliff to find not one, but two half-eaten Snickers bars in ruins on my clean floor. The plastic display case for bandanas, maps, and candy was ajar two inches. I was almost certain it had been closed when I left, and there were no guests at the hut. Caramel and milk chocolate pieces were strewn about like shrapnel. I picked up one of the chunks; it bore unmistakable, incriminating little teeth marks.

Then came the telltale screeching—was it laughter?—from atop the stove hood. I advanced on the squirrel, forensic evidence in hand. I was actually impressed, I told him (it's not uncommon for caretakers to talk to squirrels). But did he have to take two bars, and finish neither? Why not just take one, and finish the whole thing?

This logic apparently lost on him, the squirrel just looked at me, let out one last triumphant trill, and was gone.

With the cool perspective of hindsight, I now have a different interpretation of his oratory. I allow that the red squirrel has a more frank, intuitive appreciation of the entropic threat than I do. I see his "wild" behavior in a different, almost heroic light. I picture the red squirrel chattering away at the domineering universe from his metallic perch, forefeet clenched in tiny fists, echoing Dostoyevsky's bitter narrator railing against unseen deterministic forces in *Notes from the Underground*: "I am not a piano key!"

* * *

For a few days that first December my quiet evenings at Carter Notch Hut were punctured by artillery-like booms. The lake ice was caving in on itself. The lakes drained through their boulder-lined bottoms, emerging as the origins of the Wildcat River further down the mountain. As the water level dropped several feet below the surface ice, it collapsed in sections; to the uninitiated listener it sounded like the opening salvoes of a Canadian invasion. Even if you knew what it was, it was startling.

In the morning I looked out the crew-room window at the litter of house-sized chunks of granite blanketing the slopes above

—and imagined it to be the aftermath of the previous night's detonations. This field of rubble is known as The Ramparts. It's as vivid a display of dispersal that I know. A sizeable piece of Carter Dome sheared off in 1869, and the detritus settled on the southeast slopes of the Notch. Giant boulders are strewn above the hut like discarded chess pieces. The wind and water that accelerate into and through the Notch are patiently grinding them to dust, and ice helps out by cracking their seams wider. Several points for Team Entropy. (But ice caves also form between and beneath some of them. The ice lasts through the summer, perfect for keeping the universe's waste heat out of a caretaker's precious beer supply. Point for Team Notch.)

I walked to the shore of the smaller of the Carter Lakes. The ice now mirrored the jumble of The Ramparts. The once-smooth surface, perfect for one-man hockey games, now resembled broken glass remnants shoved into a wastebasket, all shards and slabs carelessly strewn and piled atop each other. It was an awesome, gloomy spectacle. There would be no more skating, and getting water would be a bit trickier. But there were signs of life. The crows cawed loudly as they trundled in a leaden sky. I saw I was not the first to investigate the disorder. The fox's prints were there too, along the shore.

9

On Being Lost

* * *

BLAIR BRAVERMAN

2011, Co-winner

Colby College, in Maine, sits atop a broad hill that slopes down into woods on all sides, like a castle moated by a tangled knot of trees. In my four years at this school, I've spent a great deal of time getting lost in these woods, whose size—only a few square miles, really—suggests that for most of us, getting lost would be difficult if not impossible. Luckily, I'm willing to put in the effort. There's a magic in being lost, and when I set off for an hour's or an afternoon's expedition, I try to cross the boundary into the unfamiliar. I try to find an instability of place.

I leave my dormitory and enter the woods along a broad, rutted-dirt trail. My favorite time to do this is early morning, when the sky is blue and the branches are dark veins against the white light of the rising sun on the horizon—or else on overcast mornings, when the whole gray sky seems to glow above me, smooth with fog or mottled with clouds, and the sun could be nowhere or everywhere at once. In fact, any time of day will do. I walk down the trail, feeling the solidity of the earth beneath my sneakers, the small variations of pebbles or roots. Within a few minutes I begin to pass animal trails, threads of open space, marked only by a slight parting of bushes, a crack of greenery less dense than that around it. It is these that I most like to follow.

Sometimes there are footprints between the ferns, footprints cloven and confident, no longer than my thumb. They are even, immaculate, each pressed into the soil with equal force; my own footprints, on the other hand, vary from the deep gouge of a landed leap to a gentle disturbance of twigs, left while I hesitate to look over my shoulder. If I were to walk with certainty, then my prints would be as the deer's; as it is, I've got no chance in the world.

Lately I've been wondering how animals navigate—if they even realize they are navigating. When a deer passed along this trail, parting these same bushes, was she following a scent, a feeling, a certain unknowable pull toward food or water or home?

I've never seen an animal lost, not outdoors at least. I've seen animals lost indoors, and I know that even to witness such a thing is alarming, disconcerting. Last year, while waiting for a flight at JFK airport in New York, I saw no fewer than four plump sparrows swooping under the domed ceiling. They rode the air in high arcs, passing over the bowed heads of men and women holding suitcases and cell phones. One of the sparrows kept fluttering against a tall window, sliding back and forth against the glass, over and around. It would stop, rest its small feet on the sill and shiver itself into a perfect light ball; then, after its feathers had smoothed, it would rise again to fly endlessly against the glass. Two of the other birds were hopping beneath a row of benches, pecking the ground. One held a worm in its beak, and I stared at it, stunned, wondering how this perfect anomaly had occurred, how a bird and worm had both happened into the same cement-walled room and found each other in time to enact this modest replica of wildness; then, at the same moment, I understood that the worm was a French fry.

I thought, then, that the birds could spend their whole lives in the airport, could find food and water and simply live there, for years, maybe even die of old age in that one room.

In any case, though the deer who made these trails may well have known its destination, I don't know mine, and that's how I want it. I don't try to lose my way; instead, I simply let myself follow, follow whims or desires or some vestigial instinct left long undeveloped and unheeded. I walk. I walk over roots and down into gullies, walk through the creases of earth worn away by last year's snowmelt, walk into and out of clearings. I pluck ticks from my ankles. I loiter, wallow, rub leaves between my fingers.

In the spring, I count fiddleheads as they sprout, admire their elegance as they push through humus in delicate curls; later, as I pass through a carpet of ferns, I remember how they started out. I lie on my back and look at the sky, then I lie on my stomach and look at the soil. I have seen squirrels, deer, skunks, groundhogs, and on one occasion, a red fox, who trotted parallel to my path for several minutes; we stared at each other the whole time, neither of us changing direction. Then, abruptly, the fox was gone, ducked and vanished into some unseen cavern, and I understood that it had come home.

Usually, after an hour or two of wandering, I too begin heading for home. Unlike the fox, I never beeline; I couldn't if I tried. I know that if I make my way uphill, I usually emerge at some point into a field, or near a road I recognize. But I have, at other times, surprised myself, coming out in a location totally, miraculously unknown. Once, blinking, I stepped out of the woods and into a groomed backyard, where I was met with three charging poodles. After a moment's consideration, I sprinted around the side of the house—which was generously pillared, with three cars in the driveway—and came panting into a cul-de-sac, which I traced back to a main road several miles from campus. Later, when I looked at a map, I discovered that the section of woods I had emerged from was not, in fact, attached to the section of woods I had entered several hours before; they were separated by a four-lane highway, which I had never actually crossed.

Do you understand? I am addicted to such mysteries.

Last summer I worked as a mapmaker for Colby's Environmental Studies program. I sat for eight hours a day in a computer lab, staring at a screen, trying to diagram Maine's woods and mountains

—trying to demystify them. It was technical work. I spent a lot of time typing numbers into spreadsheets, column after column; it was hard to imagine that data like this could somehow represent wilderness. But there was, I found, a precise beauty in the maps' layers, the speckled lakes and jagged mountains, the lacy coastline, the spiderweb of roads and rivers. I liked to know where everything was, to see the relationships between places, the way creeks converged into streams, and streams into rivers, and the thick mass of forest spread across the northern half of the state like jam on toast. And to be able to put these maps together myself, to construct a model representing hundreds of miles—I felt like I was cupping the whole state between my hands.

One morning, as I settled into the lab, my professor came to me in a rush. That very afternoon, he said, he would be bringing several researchers up into the mountains to show them a conservation project he was working on, and that they had helped to fund. He needed a map. Not just any map, but one made by his own student, in his own lab. He wanted to show them what I could do. Normally, it took me days, if not weeks, to make a map—he needed this one in three hours. Could I do it?

Of course, I told him, already starting to sweat. A map. I could do it. In three hours? No problem. Relax, I said. I have it under control.

For the rest of the morning, I typed and squinted and cursed, tracked down data and tried to make sense of it. I painted rivers. I colored the forest. I shaded the dark sides of mountains. I added a legend, a compass, and a scale bar, and I signed my name at the bottom: by Blair Braverman, June 2010. The map, when I finished, was lovely—bright and intricate, detailed enough to be useful in navigation without sacrificing artistry. I printed five copies—one for my professor and each of the researchers—then slid them into plastic covers, knocked on my professor's door, and handed him the neat stack. He smiled. My job was done.

That evening I went for a walk in the woods, and I felt a certain confidence I had never before experienced, an unfamiliar sense of authority. I know you, I thought to the trees. I had mapped the wilderness. I was on top of it.

The feeling lasted until the next day, when I met my professor with his head in his hands. How had the trip with the researchers gone? A disaster, he said—well no, not quite a disaster, but an embarrassment. He had spoken so highly of his students, and so proudly of the map I'd made, and yet when he and the researchers began to search for a certain river that was an integral part of the conservation effort, they drove in circles for over an hour; they simply could not make a connection between the map in their hands and the landscape around them. It wasn't until late in the afternoon that my professor realized, in horror, that the river wasn't on the map. I had simply—forgotten it. Left it out. How was that possible? My professor didn't know; I had used official government data. I looked at the map—but it was so pretty!—and then out the window, feeling helpless. It was windy outside, and trees waved their branches, the forest shrinking away toward the horizon.

I sat down that evening with my map and an atlas, creased flat on the table, and began to compare the two, segment by segment. Sure enough, there was the river in the atlas, and when I looked at my own map, I couldn't even find the place where it was supposed to be. The only thing there was a lake—a really big lake. The lake wasn't named, and—now, this was strange—I couldn't find it in the atlas. In fact, it seemed to be directly covering the missing river—and not just that but the whole area around it, a dozen or so small towns, two mountains.

I stared at the map and atlas with a feeling of dawning horror. It was possible, I realized, that I had drowned half of northern Maine.

Later, I would think that the amazing thing wasn't the lake itself, but the fact that none of us had noticed it. Not me, not my professor, not even the researchers—we had all failed to question a lake the size of a Rhode Island puddled in the middle of the state, a lake none of us had ever heard of. That even as the researchers searched the map for a certain river, it was easier to acknowledge it as missing than to point out that Hey, so's the rest of the county! After all, the data should have been reliable. The computer shouldn't have lied.

This was the first time that being lost frightened me.

I thought of the sparrows in the airport, nesting in the branches of potted trees, swallowing French fries. I thought about how they could live their whole lives in that terminal, cocooned in glass and cement, soaring under metal beams. Did they even realize something was missing? Did I?

A sparrow, I have learned, navigates with the direction of the setting sun, the angle of the horizon in the distance. A beaver builds its home based on the flow of water, and measures the seasons not by weeks or months but by the chill of the air, by the crust of ice that starts at the edges of the pond and spreads inward, a silver ceiling. A bat echolocates, a grasshopper follows the prevailing winds, a bear lets its nose find the way.

And I pass through a doorway into the bright outside, down a path to the mouth of the woods. I step off-trail, walk through a crease in the bushes, follow the shadows of mountains cast by a sun 93 million miles away. There's a chipmunk on a stump, ignoring me, and a line of ants by my feet. The wind is still. I take a few turns; I've never been here before. At the top of a hill, I stop to catch my breath and look out at the horizon, over fields and the dark roofs of a few loose cabins. Far beyond them, in the distance, is the flash of sunlight on a lake.

10

The Warp and Weft

* * *

BETHANY TAYLOR

2011, Co-winner

 I write this from my house in Jackson, feet propped on the windowsill while the Ellis River rushes below. From here, the sound of the water is like distant laughter. The confluence of the Ellis and Wildcat Brook borders my yard. Most days, the presence of the water is as ordinary as the garage. But other times—better times—the weight of the rivers' course leaves me breathless. These rivers first burst open with snowmelt more years ago than I can ever know and will continue to do so long after I am gone, the water eternally rising and falling with the rains and seasons.

In the rare, crystalline moments when I fully witness forces larger than myself, chills run down my spine and I recognize life as good and sweet and full. I find a scrap of this grace in a certain slant of light coming down at sunset across the alpine zone, jagged rocks the colors of gold and iron. I hear the same in the thrum of the ocean, crashing new waves in a timeless pattern across the sands. The clarity of the stars on dark nights slices to the core of this like a paring knife through an apple. All of these things—either thought or witnessed—are so ordinary as to be comforting yet so primal as to be sublime. It is in the balance of these moments, when I am at once held in place and sprung free from, aware of, my own limits of being that I feel most alive. Alive, and blessedly insignificant. To be aware of all that is greater than myself, to see for a moment the enormity of time, of seasons, and the capacity of the world to beat on, endlessly, as if past and future mean nothing, this is where I find what some might call wildness, what others might call holiness or beauty or truth. It does not matter what we call this when we find it—the sensation goes deeper than words anyway.

Think, if you will, of your life as a thread being pulled through the fabric of time. I do not know how large the fabric is. The color of your thread, the shape of the line you stitch, and who or what might be pulling the thread, I don't care much about either. Hold faith in those details as you choose. I see my thread as long and the stitches perhaps uneven, but I will, always, eventually pierce through the fabric and pull tight against it, again and again. The moments when I sense the holy-wildness of the world, and my own brief presence within it, are the times when my own thread pulls tight, when I am both joined to and apart from the fabric of time and space. These are the times I feel most alive, for I begin to sense how limited and precious my time here truly is.

A friend told me of a poet who gave his wife old bones and bird skulls as love letters. I can think of few things as sweet. "Life," the bones say, "is transient and fragile. We will all decay, but here, here while we are so briefly alive, you and I are together in this moment of time." This is almost what these wild-holy times of beauty say as well. To me, these instances of reckoning with the finite nature of being human, the reality that you've got less than a century here, are sweetly galvanizing. Better make the short time here, under the stars and along the rivers, amid the forests and atop the mountains, better make it good. So say the bones and rocks and stars. Listen.

There is no place on earth I find more storied, poetic, or beautiful than the Crawford Path, above treeline and at sunset. In the right company, it is all that I might find wild and holy. I've been there many times and cannot get enough of it. Looking toward the sinking summer sun, the mountains to the west unfold and unfold and the gold light kisses the green of the trees and turns them purple and blue. I lift up my arms in the evening breeze, over my head, and feel the air on my skin. I hear the ripple of the wind against my body. It is always, almost, the same—more or less, these are the same winds that sweep across these mountains, these rocks and plants and occasional people, every day and have since the rocks were formed in these familiar and well-loved shapes. The molecules of it all are never the same, of course, but the patterns, the sweep and flow of air, these are part of a timeless dance. And just now, just for the moment when I disturb the air and the wind accommodates my movement, I am part of it all. That my disturbance is so small, that the wind and the rocks and the setting sun and the gold and purple glow of the moment are so constant and all encompassing, this is enough to remind me of my insignificance, my mortality, and the wild-holy happenstance of my own existence. My heartbeat and breath change, and I wish the smile on my face could stretch as wide as my arms, as wide as the landscape.

In Thornton Wilder's play, *Our Town*, his Emily cries out a farewell to the world that I wish I had the faith to greet each morning with. "Oh earth," she says, "you're too wonderful for anybody to realize you. Do any human beings ever realize life while they live it?—every, every minute?" "No," another character replies. "The saints and poets, maybe—they do some."

When I watch the sun go down the craggy shoulders of the Presidential Range, the orange glow running toward the Greens and Adirondacks, I may come closest to realizing life.

What humbles me is that I used to think that the earth was only wonderful far from people and paved roads. Wildness was solely the province of the green areas on maps and only in such isolation could I feel the threads of being snap taut and awake. My environmentalism, my ethics and way of being, was never anything but selfish. I wanted, in the marrow of my bones, to preserve the places —mostly mountaintops and shorelines of New England—where I had begun to realize life, where I had first become conscious of my thread squeezing through the warp and weft of time. I felt my best self in wild places—the sad and frightened parts of myself melted away in the face of wildness. I was afraid that without wild spaces I would come apart, unstitched like a rag doll.

To hold wildness, I imagined my life going in the way of a hermit-explorer. I would go farther and deeper and wilder from the mainstream culture that was choking the rivers and bringing toxic rain to the mountains. So I dreamed of islands and mountain cabins, longing to pull far and farther away. But I began to know and know of men and women who died in pursuit of the same, to feel the wide nets of grief that catch loved ones like minnows and my longing for isolation tempered. I clung to my familiar landscapes as a life raft —they would be my wilderness, my only source of wildness. Still believing that the salvation of, if not the world then certainly myself, lay in wildness, I needed and asked everything from these few places. I did not believe that any sort of true wild beauty could lie outside the boundary lines.

And then, several years ago, far from my beloved and known New England wilds, I drove through Portland, Oregon. A bridge spanned the Willamette River and caught the fading sunlight in rusty steel trusses and brown-stained cement, lit this old industrial structure with the exact key of gold-light as I find in the mountains of home. Alone in a creaking car and gridlocked in rush hour traffic, to find beauty at all was as unexpected as a valentine in August. Let alone for the beautiful thing to be so opposite and foreign to my ideals of beauty, of wildness. And yet . . . there is my heartbeat and breath and the tug of a thread, all just as if I were in the mountains. If I could take my hands off the wheel and stretch toward the bridge, I would. Rather than the timelessness of the rocks on a trail, I thought of the rivets in the bridge, of the mortality of tough and fragile men who built the bridge, whose hands had maneuvered the cranes and placed the beams. I did not know their history, and judging by the red-gold of the rusty bridge, their time passed years ago. But here I was, seeing the same sun as ever hit the same bridge, and I felt small and safely lodged in the vast fabric of time and space. How could I have lived my life, ignoring the chances for beauty and wildness outside of wild places?

The poet Frank O'Hara's tombstone reads, "Grace to be born and live as variously as possible." I hear those words when I find wildness in strange corners. I whisper them to remind myself to look. The words, and imagining a hand carving the words into a poet's headstone, are a scrap-smile of wildness unto themselves.

T. S. Eliot writes, "We shall not cease from exploration / And the end of all our exploring / Will be to arrive where we started / And know the place for the first time." [1]

The wildness of other places and odder corners does not diminish the sublimity of my original landscapes. Rather, each time I see the most familiar places and again find in them both tonic and sanctuary, I also hold small pieces of the other times and places of wildness in my heart and the pulling of the thread through time sounds like a symphony, deepened with the wealth of instruments.

Sometimes I think that if we got rid of all protected land, all wildernesses and national forests and parks, that might be a good thing—perhaps we would learn to value all land, rather than lionizing certain geographies while destroying others. And that would be a worthy goal. A sort of land-use golden rule, do unto this landscape as you would do unto the land you most love. Perhaps we may grow to that ethos. But, for now, I see the need and merit for such designations and protections. For all that I believe with every fiber of my being that there is the possibility of wildness, of beauty, of sanctity in even the ugliest places, I still hold wilderness and remote, untrammeled landscapes dear. We need, as a people, space in which to conduct our explorations. We crave the sublime cliffs and roiling waters and distant stars to shock us awake, to open our eyes to what has always been here, what will be here after we are merely bones and dust. In wilderness, we learn to see wildness, to feel beauty. The trick is to bring those sharpened senses back from the woods, home to the mundane, and be pierced by wildness into realizing the sublime wonder in every, every minute of our briefly stitched lives.

NOTE

1   From Section V of "Little Gidding," in *Four Quartets* (New York: Harcourt Brace, 1943).

11

A Place for Everything

* * *

KATHERINE DYKSTRA

2012, Winner

 We'd thrown the trip together in a flurry of phone calls and email exchanges all in forty-eight hours. Parker researched state parks, campgrounds, driving times. Ann went to a dollar store and bought four nylon camping chairs. I went to Target and came away with two tents. There was a moment when we nearly called the whole thing off, Seth having phoned every rental car company in the five boroughs and coming up dry; it was Fourth of July weekend after all. But dogged in his pursuit, he eventually found a car that had been returned early. It was the last, we believed, in the city.

As we inched our way west on Canal Street, Seth caught my eye in the rearview mirror: "So I hear you're worried about bears," he said, amused.

Ann, tiny and brunette, twisted around in her seat and smiled at me in the same way an adult might smile at a child who simply didn't know any better. I felt myself turn red. As we'd made our preparations to flee the city, I happened to notice that nearly every page of the Delaware Water Gap website mentioned the area's disproportionate population of black bears. But when I'd brought this to Parker's attention—"Um, do you think we'll be mauled by bears?"—he'd laughed, "That's what you're worried about? Bears? There won't be any bears. And anyway, I'll be there to protect you." After he said this, he puffed up his chest and ape-walked toward me, catching me in his arms.

The website had included a twenty-item checklist of things to do to ensure a bear did not find his way to your campsite as well as instructions for what to do if he did. When I persisted, suggesting we keep our food in the trunk of our car, tie our trash up in a tree, Parker had said, "OK, how about this? You can be our resident bear expert." At which point I knew to proceed was to risk catching a lot of flak later.

Looking straight-faced at Seth in the rearview mirror, I lied, "I'm not worried." Outside the car, a man dug through a trashcan while tourists swarmed around him. "I just wanted to make sure we were taking the right precautions." I said this in my best Little Miss Perfect voice, hoping to convey that I knew worrying about bears was ridiculous. I was, however, quite worried. When I was young, my father had taken my brother and me on weeklong camping trips to the Rocky Mountains, but this was the first time I'd been camping as an adult. And while as a child it never occurred to me that there was anything my father couldn't protect me from, as an adult, I knew that when a man and nature collided on nature's turf, nature usually won.

"Well," said Seth, "I've been camping hundreds of times and I've never seen a bear." I knew that taking this line of discussion any further would do nothing for me. This trip was supposed to be fun. We were getting out of the city. Worrying about bears was a downer. I let it go.

Which was doable, as I was choosing to take heart in the fact that that morning, before we'd left, Parker had done nature a favor, not an easy feat in a city where nature barely exists. He had been out on the fire escape when he spotted a bird, hanging upside down in a tree and frantically flapping her wings to no avail. "I have to help her," he'd said, after pointing her out to me. "Right?" He looked unsure, like he might have wanted me to stop him, but then dragged the ladder out anyway. I watched from our second-floor window as he hauled himself onto the fence that separated our apartment building from the backyard of the brownstone behind us and then climbed up into the tree. His position, clinging to one branch, was precarious and I worried for him as I watched all the birds in the neighborhood, likely fearing their friend's safety, circle him like warplanes, one even clipping him on the ear. When he finally came back inside, he told me that the bird had managed to tie her foot to a tree branch with some dental floss, likely while building her nest. He'd untied her from the tree and then held her in one gloved hand while he untied the floss from her leg.

A couple years before—pre-Parker—in another apartment, I'd awakened one morning to an amazing clatter. Sitting up in bed I found myself eye to eye with a baby pigeon that appeared to have crash-landed on my air conditioning unit, presumably while attempting first flight. He stood there shaking, a ball of downy fluff and feathers, four stories up with panic in his eyes. I wanted to help him but I didn't know how; I was afraid of him in the same way I was afraid of the stray cats in my Brooklyn neighborhood; what if he had something? "Having something," being the way my mother has warned me away from wildlife all my life, as in, "Don't touch that kitten! It might have something." And so my pigeon stayed there, beak-to-glass, until I left for work. On the way to the subway, I called my landlord and told him about the bird, asked what I should do. He seemed unsure and said to leave it up to him. When I got home that evening, the bird was gone. I feared it had plummeted to its death. A friend tried to comfort me with the words *natural selection*. Parker, I thought in the car, would have tried to save it.

We four arrived at Dingman's Campground inside the park with just enough time to pitch the tents before night fell. It had been a mad dash, but we'd done it. We sat around the campfire covertly drinking beer (the campsite was dry), idealistically talking about stories we wanted to tell, films we wanted to make. Anything seemed possible from the vantage point of our small success. At a reasonable hour we turned in, set on rising early the next day.

But once in the tent, the good feeling was gone, and I couldn't sleep. Wedged into the angle where the forest floor met a snoring Parker, my ears were sharp for any sound. I listened hard to the night, trying to distinguish the difference between plant-life rustling in the wind, acorns falling onto the tarp, and the footfalls of an animal keen on ripping our tent apart with its teeth. When the sun rose, I was already awake, feeling as if I hadn't slept at all.

But the day dawned bright and beautiful, reminding me, once again, that this was fun. And it was. We cooked bacon and eggs over the fire for breakfast. We took off on a two-hour hike that ended at a waterfall, swam in the Delaware River, and fished from the shore. Back at camp that evening, we ate burgers on buns with onions and barbeque sauce, potatoes roasted with peppers, baked beans, everything slightly burned. Lounging around the campfire with river water in our hair, it felt good. Like we'd won.

I cracked a beer, tipped my head back, and was surprised to find that up through the pines, tall as buildings over our heads, the sky was still day-blue. Shadows had crept in along the ground as we'd cooked. Looking back, this is likely why we didn't notice him until he was right up on us.

"Oh my god," said Parker, in a low voice that betrayed both astonishment and fear, and made me look up immediately. At first he looked like the big black dog we'd seen racing after a stick earlier that day, but this guy was bulkier, wide as a wheelbarrow, and he moved slowly like a monster patiently taking a city.

"We're going to get up, and we're going to walk away."

I felt proud of how quickly Parker had seized control of the situation, but for some reason I couldn't move, my eyes fixed on the bear, waiting to see what he would do.

"Now!" Parker hissed. "We are all going to get up, and we're going to walk away." This time I stood. And kind of walk/skipped through the trees to the adjacent campsite where a middle-aged couple had just pulled out a pair of pork chops.

"There's a bear in our campsite," I whispered, realizing I'd abandoned all my stuff. I envisioned the bear ransacking our tents, devouring my iPhone, my camera, in a fit of rage.

"Yup," said the man, barely looking up. "I see 'im."

"You can get in our van if you like," the man's lady friend offered. I straightened at their nonchalance, turned around.

Rather than bury his face in the picnic table covered in half-eaten bags of chips, green salsa, and packages of hot dogs and buns, he ambled right up to the tree where we'd tied up our trash. After a moment of what looked like thought, he expertly stood on his hind legs, rested one paw against the trunk of the tree, and gently took the bag off the rope we'd tied it to. He then sauntered away over the hill, holding the trash as if he were taking it out.

Ann turned to me her eyes the size of salad plates. "I have never seen a bear while camping before!" She gripped my forearm, as if to say, *Please believe me!* As if I thought that, in an attempt to alleviate my fear, she'd lied the day before. I did believe her. But that was beside the point. More than fear, now I felt satisfaction. My worry had been warranted.

We deliberated for a moment—bear, campsites, children—and decided it was best to alert the ranger, and so Seth and Ann took our rental car to the lodge. Not a moment after they pulled away, Parker and I watched as the bear lumbered back into view at a campsite across the way. He stopped in front of a picnic table draped in mosquito netting.

"Ohhh," said Parker, with the same laughing inflection he uses when he watches something explode on TV. "He's going to destroy that thing!"

He had dug out my camera and was clicking away in the bear's direction. I felt giddy too, in the daylight and at a distance; I was ready to see some destruction. But the show was not spectacular. After shifting his weight back and forth for a moment, the bear merely walked on to the next site and then the site after that until he'd walked out of view, at which point we saw a girl run quickly in the other direction. I was disappointed to see him go, both because I wanted to keep an eye on him—he was frightening, the size of a pedicab, and with all that pent-up power roiling through his body—and because I was hypnotized by him, by his beauty—sleek black coat, onyx eyes, and velvet nose. I knew I had just witnessed something special, something I might never see again. But he didn't come back, and all was quiet until Seth and Ann returned with the rangers.

Parker and I pointed them in the right direction. After they'd pulled away, Ann frantically began cleaning up the picnic table, throwing everything half-eaten into a new trash bag, which she then shook in her outstretched hand at Seth: "This was what he wanted; I don't want it here." She said this with wide eyes and a smile, mocking her own panic, but was totally serious. Seth shrugged, "I'll take it to the Dumpster." I offered to join him, jumping at the chance to use an actual toilet—there was one at the entrance to the campground.

When we got there, we ran, once again, into the bear. He was stumbling through the forest and turning at odd angles. He seemed confused; when we stopped the car, rolled down the windows, I understood why. The rangers had driven their truck into the trees and were charging him with lights on, sirens blaring. One ranger, who barely fit in his uniform, yelled through a megaphone alternately at the bear: "Please leave our campsite! We are asking you nicely!" and at the crowd of campers who had assembled behind him: "Back away! This bear is aggressive! He charged me! I'm not kidding!"

Another ranger got out of the truck carrying a long thin rifle. I looked at Seth, raised my eyebrows.

"It's a tranquilizer gun," said Seth, one wrist hooked over the steering wheel. "They'll knock him out and drop him off somewhere else so he can't find his way back."

The energy of the crowd outside our car had reached a frenzy.

The fat ranger was now more concerned with keeping back a group of half-clad twenty-somethings falling all over themselves in excitement than he was with the bear behind him. I looked at the small dark shape turning circles in the trees amid the flashing lights and the tinny screech of the bullhorn, and felt an overwhelming sadness.

Seth rolled his eyes. "Idiots," he said. We dumped our trash, headed back to our campsite.

Seth and I told Parker and Ann what we'd seen. We all wondered what the rangers would do, what would become of the bear. Seth pointed out that he had seen a tag in the bear's ear, which likely meant that the bear had entered a campsite before. We agreed the bear was young, not a cub, but maybe a tween, and we wondered whether his mother would come looking for him later. And when we were done talking about that, we sat in uneasy silence in the growing dark. As if suddenly we were unsure of our business there between those trees.

We stayed up late that night. We watched as all points of light around our site were gradually snuffed out until it was just us crouched around our campfire, a glowing circle in the infinite dark. We roasted and ate an entire package of hot dogs. We told stories of camping when we were kids, but didn't quite listen to one another. We drank Jameson out of a water bottle and killed an entire case of beer, tossing our crushed empties in a pile on the ground, so different from the night before when we took care to hide them in our tents, open them under a cough, pour them in the shadows. The night before there had been a circling car, a ranger we assumed on the lookout. Tonight he was gone. We were alone. It was as if the rules no longer applied.

Seth passed out in his chair and when he woke up again, he convinced us that eating the second package of hot dogs was a good idea. Parker, drunk, tried to engage us in a sing-along we'd once done at a party in LA, but the mood was so different. I had managed to drink myself sober, alert in my nylon chair.

A Place for Everything

By 3:00 a.m., we were all spent and ready for it to be over, but early on, Seth had put a four-foot-long log onto the fire; it still hadn't burned into the pit, and Parker insisted we wait up until the log fit.

"Everything must be contained in the pit," he slurred. "That is the rule, everything has to be contained."

I understood his meaning. There are certain rules one has to follow when a guest in the wild. We needed to follow those rules, to finish what we had started. I thought perhaps if we did, everything would be OK.

Seth and Ann sat in their chairs, heads rolled back, sometimes speaking, while I stood over the flame, maniacally twisting the log into the heart of the fire as Parker knelt before it and blew.

When we finally crawled into our tents, I lay on my back, the beer buzzing in my ears, and wondered what the rangers had done with the bear. I wasn't afraid anymore. Instead, I felt a part of the forest around me.

The next morning, hungover, slow-moving, almost ashamed, we broke down the tents, packed up the car. We put the rest of the food—potatoes, eggs, bacon—all together in one pot, cooked it and called it cowboy mash. I had one bite. It made me want to throw up. Then we went to the lodge to check out.

"What happened with the bear last night?" I asked the woman behind the counter as she stabbed a calculator with her pointer finger.

"He got aggressive, and he wouldn't leave the campground, so they had to kill him," she said, without looking at me.

My stomach sank. "They killed him?"

"He was aggressive and he wouldn't leave the campground."

"Of course he was aggressive," said a leathery man who stood on the other side of the register. "You were chasing him."

"He was aggressive," she repeated.

I walked outside carrying the weight of what we had done.

"They killed him," I said to the other three.

"I will never come back here again," said the grizzled wife of the leathery man as she came down the steps of the lodge. "He wasn't aggressive. We were the first people to see him at our campsite; he just walked in. I got my camera!"

We got back in our car and sat silent. All I could think is that we had left the city, come out to the country, shot a bear, and now we were going home.

"It wasn't our fault," Ann said from the back seat.

"Yeah, he was tagged," Seth said. "It was only a matter of time."

"I know," I said. And I did. And yet.

When we told the story to our friends, families, coworkers, they said that there was an overpopulation of bears in that area, that the rangers had to kill him to protect the site. And of course, I didn't want the bear to have hurt anyone. But if the rangers were protecting the site, my question was, Who was protecting the bear?

I flashed on a summer day when my brother John and I had arrived at my mother's house in North Carolina at the same time a man from animal control was ridding the attic of a nest of bats. As they swooped out of the house over our heads, hundreds of black shapes filling the air above us with flapping wings and little screams, one fell to the concrete in front of me. The Bat Man picked it up by the tips of its wings, and showed it to me—little fangs and beady blinking eyes—I shrunk away, "Ew."

"Aw," said John, gently. "He's just trying to be a bat."

12

Wilderness

* * *

ANGELA ZUKOWSKI

2012, Runner-up

As dusk dropped down over a sylvan Georgia hollow on my very first night on the Appalachian Trail, an old man stuck his head out of his tent to greet me. "I was expecting something with a bit more wilderness," he said plaintively. I chuckled to myself as the man retreated back inside his tent and zipped it closed, preserving his illusion of solitude. I suppose I was just as naïve. When I imagined myself on the Appalachian Trail, it had always been in the context of the rugged, unyielding, and harsh beauty of New England.

As my long-distance hike continued I spent much of the trail yearning for Vermont, New Hampshire, and Maine, wondering why there were so many switchbacks and gentle trails and where all the rocks were hiding. Like the old man on my inaugural night, I wanted a more pure wilderness and the trail just didn't feel wild enough. Though unaware at the time, I wanted the wildness to temper me into a better version of myself. When that failed to happen it was much easier to blame the hike instead of blaming myself. It took me over a thousand miles of walking and the rugged beauty of New Hampshire and Maine to convince me to love the Appalachian Trail unconditionally. But something still felt lacking.

When my hike was completed, I felt I had tempered my inexperience on the granddaddy of all trails and was ready for the next step in my wilderness experience. I was hired as a backcountry caretaker in the summer of 2011 with the Appalachian Mountain Club. The glorious days spent on ridgelines in the White Mountains as I thru-hiked had convinced me: New Hampshire was calling. Perhaps there I'd find that hidden element at the crux of a true wilderness experience, on the trails that left even seasoned thru-hikers bruised and shaky, exhausted and humbled.

New Hampshire native Daniel Webster stated: "Men hang out their signs indicative of their respective trades; shoe makers hang out a gigantic shoe; jewelers a monster watch, and the dentist hangs out a gold tooth; but up in the Mountains of New Hampshire, God Almighty has hung out a sign to show that there He makes men." While I didn't fit the definition by gender, I had visions of becoming a hardened woodswoman, worthy of Mr. Webster's criteria. The type who didn't even break a sweat striding up slide trails or maneuvering blowdowns. Who bushwhacked before breakfast and navigated wherever she pleased. The type of person the average day hiker would look at and instantly feel intimidated by. I would exude rugged wilderness from my very pores; the ax I was issued during my first days of training was proof of this.

Nauman Tentsite sits quietly beside Mizpah Spring Hut on a stretch of the White Mountains known as the Presidential Range. Thru-hikers and day hikers alike find themselves catching their breath on the steep ascent up Webster Cliffs. The venerable Crawford Path leads unerringly to the pleasant dome of Mount Eisenhower before pushing onward to greater heights. The quiet patches of bog tucked away on sides of mountains and the mossy byways lining elderly trails gently give way to the rock-littered slopes of Washington, Jefferson, Adams, and Madison. Brimming with anticipation, I packed my backpack with ten days' worth of food, my ax, and various odds and ends, then staggered up the Crawford Path for the first of many times that summer.

Each night in my tent I pored over my map, tracing the segments marked "Wilderness" and "National Forest." At first I diligently planned hikes in the most rugged-sounding places I could come up with: Isolation Mountain, the Dry River Wilderness, the Great Gulf Wilderness. I tore past startled day hikers as I ran down the Crawford Path, determined to make each endeavor epic. I would be faster, stronger, and bolder than all the other hikers. I would carve my own wilderness out of the centuries-old bridle path.

But it didn't work. The more I sought solitude, the more I encountered others just like me. On a beautiful balmy day you could find hikers sunning themselves on every summit, as if at the beach. From each peak I'd see a string of tiny ants crawling inexorably toward me, a flood of hikers inundating the krummholz with itineraries and enthusiasm. Hiking toward Mount Washington was akin to making your way down a crowded school corridor; dodging left and right, passing the dawdlers, edging your way past backpacks and clumps of chattering people. Mornings were punctuated with both birdsong and hollers from children; evenings closed not with silent forests, but with garrulous conversations penetrating the thin walls of my tent. If an escape from fellow man was a part of the definition of wilderness, then it certainly was not to be found on the trails of the Presidential Range.

I soon realized I wasn't becoming a modern-day Daniel Boone while living in my tent in the woods. I was instead becoming soft, less inclined to bushwhack, more likely dropping in on Mizpah each morning for socialization and scones, a morning ritual that defied my original purpose. I needed to get off-trail, I decided. It was the trails that were ruining my wilderness experience. The trails and the huts and the tentsites: all were to blame. Easy culprits for sure, teeming with people, with no escape in sight.

And so I left the trails and struck out into the woods. I found where moose trod next to the Crawford Path. I swam in swimming holes as hikers strode past just yards away, unaware of my presence. I crouched in hidden nooks of blowdowns, woodland parlors with moss cushions, and stared out at secret views of far-off peaks. I tried to find old-growth forest, and scat, and the remains of logging camps, but still I remained disheartened, as I came to the conclusion that there would always be others who were bolder than I, more competent, more immersed in wilderness. It wasn't the location or the people surrounding me that delineated my limitations, but myself.

The word "wilderness" derives from the concept of "wildness," that which is not controllable by humans. However, the presence of people does not disqualify an area from being wilderness. Slowly I began to accept that but I still struggled with letting go of this almost mystical vision. My idealized version of wilderness was something I still yearned for, yet could not articulate.

Wilderness has been an inscrutable algorithm to me. One that I longed to solve in the hope that it would mold me into a better person, a stronger-willed, more knowledgeable, more capable human being. It evolved into a Holy Grail characterized by vast expanses of land devoid of humanity. It loomed in the distance, attainable only by those who threw themselves at its harsh mercy. It attracted a certain kind of person, a strange elite exemplified by hardiness, endurance, solitude, and stoic suffering.

I strained to join this rare breed, restrained by my suburban upbringing, ignorance, excuses, and an occasional dash of laziness. Sitting in my damp chilly canvas tent with the hoots of other peoples' garrulous festivities punctuating my summer evenings, I pored over books I'd thumbed through many times before. In most of them, the protagonists were men. In my eyes they had achieved the rarified glory of accomplishing things that few others were hardened enough to suffer through. They had penetrated wilderness and made it their own. Wilderness was untamed by humanity, likewise these men. They summited mountains, lived off the land, survived unthinkable hardships and endured the fickle accidents that nature tended to throw at random into their paths: avalanches, storms, hypothermia, altitude sickness. If I could do this too, if I could thrive in the sort of harsh environment that most of the civilized world shunned or was afraid of, I would accomplish something tangibly better than my current existence. There was some sort of vague equation in my mind that went something like this: landscape untouched by humans plus epic deed equals true wilderness equals a valid self. And yet all summer as I read I secretly knew that this would never be me.

I might never venture to a vast tract of land untouched by people. I was perhaps slightly more knowledgeable than the average hiker, thanks to my training for this job as a caretaker and many months of living outdoors, but I was never going to magically turn into one of those heroic characters who struck off on her own and accomplished bold things in places like the Yukon or Hindustan. At the rate I was going, I wasn't even going to accomplish bold things in New England. Wilderness had become a loaded term for me, one heavy with personal meaning. My vision of it was inextricably linked with my own capability in the natural world. It was so much easier for me to capitulate to insecurity and self-criticism by creating an impossible definition for wilderness and competency. Deep down though, I was tired of yearning for something that was out of my reach.

I finally acknowledged that there was no button I could press that would instantly mold me into a rugged explorer and I accepted the fact that perhaps the mountains of New Hampshire and Maine were the only form of wilderness I'd encounter for much of my life. I realized that this wasn't necessarily a bad thing. I let go of any notion that epic accomplishments were what mattered in the wilderness and I began instead to appreciate what I truly was skilled at doing outdoors: observing. Maybe, just maybe, in spite of my weakness for baked goods and my amateurish skill with an ax, I was good enough. I was worthy of this environment and it deserved my full appreciation. There was no need to conquer or dominate or achieve anything other than that.

Now there are memories that flood me with peace and that

still, even today, cause me to catch my breath. Recollections that can sweep me back to a place and make me feel as though my feet are still planted on that earth in that moment, though it may have passed months ago. There are sensations and emotions triggered not by events or people but by sky and sun, clouds and wind, trees, moss, lichen. A smile triggered by a raven arcing through a chalcedony-blue winter sky, cawing indifferently as I watch below from my perch on an icy outcropping. A quiet moment of peace just moments away from a busy White Mountain tentsite, standing in a perfect circular hollow of moss. Reveling in the singular beauty of a sunrise in the White Mountains, bold rich color viewed through the starkly delineated silhouettes of trees just below an alpine summit. Hiking up the ordinarily well-trafficked Crawford Path on a foggy dreary day and not encountering a single soul, the quiet magnified by the deep cushions of damp moss surrounding me. Watching droplets of water converge and swell as they trace the lines of hobblebush leaves after a rainy morning. Walking outside on a night when temperatures are plummeting below zero and staring upward, wondering why the cold seems to make the silent star-filled sky seem impossibly crystalline, almost on the verge of shattering. Breathing in the scent of evergreen needles and listening to the thrum of grouse wings as birds take flight. Soaking in sunlight in the krummholz, napping on an unyielding, ancient granite surface. These things are what truly matter and I was foolish to ever dismiss them in pursuit of bigger and bolder things. If I want wilderness untouched by man, all I need to do is marvel at a tiny pebble or a lace doily of lichen on a boulder; the enduring existence of both in the rugged White Mountains far exceeds the scope of mankind.

We can't all escape to a truly pristine landscape devoid of humanity. But we can open our eyes to what is around us. We can shed some of our more civilized urges and needs and desires and embrace ones that are a little more primitive. We can celebrate the wild joy that floods the heart when you discover and embrace the wilderness in your surroundings. I am reminded of the old man I met at the beginning of my journey. If I could go back in time, I would say to him: "This is it. Look where you are. The wilderness is all around you." Though it took many miles, I finally found that wilderness had been there all along, waiting to be joyfully shared.

13

Where the Trail Ends

* * *

WENDY UNGAR

2012

 I returned to the summit of Lookout Mountain in the summer of 2008. Its massive stone face loomed over the forest and lake below just as it had when Jane and I stood upon it more than a decade before. I sat down and once again pressed my fingers against the rough surface of the warm rock. I didn't look out to the lake below. Instead, I looked in and recalled how difficult it had been to find our way to the top— the repeated failed attempts, the obstacles that were thrown in our path.

How can a trail become so disconnected from a mountain? How can our friendship stay connected to my life? Lookout gave me no answers that day. Jane was dead but the mountain was still here and so was I. I sat upon the summit remembering.

The journey started when I looked up from my bowl of cereal one morning in 1994 with the distinct feeling that someone was watching me through the picture window.

You again.

It was that face—the face of Lookout Mountain, its peak kissing the sky without shame. I stared back. Unlike its famous cousins, the High Peaks of New York's Adirondack range, Lookout does not want to be found, let alone climbed, despite its inviting name. And here it was staring at me, just as it always had, through the kitchen window of our family summer home on Loon Lake. I felt it had something to tell me.

I decided the time had come to climb Lookout. I had to prepare properly for a journey that would take me up a mountain too obscure to be mentioned in any of the Adirondack trail guides. So I called up Jane, my faithful friend and hiking companion. Jane and I had met a few years earlier on an Adirondack Mountain Club High Peaks traverse. We quickly discovered our compatibility: in the pace we chose to maneuver the rocks and roots along the forest trail, as well as in the uneven trail of our personal and professional lives as single thirty-something academics.

"Jane, I have the perfect hike for us this summer. We can practice our map and compass skills."

"Love it," Jane replied. "Where are we going?"

"We are going to conquer Lookout Mountain."

Conquer—what an audacious word. As if anyone could hope to understand a mountain, to grasp the divine intention that placed the mountains and us here together, let alone conquer it. There are those who try to conquer mountains, to cross a name off a list, and eventually earn a badge. And then there are those who prefer to have the mountain conquer them—to have its beauty and enormity, its mystery and its secrets, invade and envelop. Jane was one of those.

Hiking with Jane meant hiking with Mollie. One-quarter black Lab, one-quarter border collie, and two-quarters crazy, Mollie was just as avid as Jane and me. Although we loved to discover new trails, Jane and I were not peakbaggers. It was normal for Jane to stop on the trail to feel the texture of an unusual mushroom, poke her nose at a flower growing in the crack of a rotting log, or catch and release a tiny tree toad that happened to hop by. It was Jane who taught me how to pack the essentials for a day hike. Besides water, food, first-aid kit, knife, topographical map, and compass, a pack was not complete without a copy of the bible. And it had to be Peterson's version. By the frayed look of Jane's copy of *A Field Guide to Wildflowers: Northeastern and North-Central North America*, by Roger Tory Peterson, she had already identified every flower and still she hauled it, along with Peterson's guide to birds and, sometimes, to mushrooms. Nature guides were her testaments and the woods her temple. And Jane treated this temple with reverence—she was its steward and guardian. If a trail was wet, I might tramp through the ferns and hobblebush that grew along the edges, but not Jane. Not wanting to cause erosion, Jane would happily stomp through the mud ponds that formed in the middle of the trail, even if it meant losing her boot. She respected the forest and its sacred earth. I believe she would have chosen it for eternity.

So late one August morning we set off to find Lookout. Most people who hike in these parts know that seeing a mountain and finding it are two different things. Finding just the right access point is key. Even for mountains with trails, you might spend hours looking for that blaze of faded blue painted on a pine tree past the meadow over a hill three miles from the creek that crosses the dirt track off a county side road. And with that elusive sign, you begin your ascent to another place.

Our region of the Adirondacks was and still is an area of active logging. It's not unusual to see trucks heavy with timber careening around the corners of back roads and know that a little bit more of the forest has been taken. The woods that are left are laced with tracks and trails that loop and stretch, ending suddenly somewhere and usually nowhere. I love to walk in these woods and get to know the trails, to know where each curve rises and falls, disappearing suddenly and starting up again a hundred yards away. I love to know the woods and for the woods to know me—to accept me and grant me access.

Looking at the topo map, Lookout rose from the contour lines in shades of brown and green like a worn and lumpy quilt. Walking paths, jeep trails, rail beds, and logging roads were stitched into the mountain with the same authority as true north. Wilderness areas are not supposed to change. And topo maps, rarely updated, are meant to be steadfast. But who knew what was left of the human-made tracks. A trail could become disconnected from a mountain and just end, seemingly for no reason. But we needed a place to start. The map showed a dirt road off County Route 99 that ended with three houses. An old jeep trail extending from a corner in the dirt road would take us close to the base of the mountain. From there, following a compass bearing of 63 degrees north-northwest should lead us to the summit. So off we went, our limbs covered in lightweight sleeves and pants. Jane was five foot two at most, but her presence was larger. It may have been from the way her citronella ablutions overwhelmed the air around her. Jane refused to use chemical mosquito repellants. Looking back now I wonder about her religious avoidance of chemicals—did it matter?

On the road, Mollie bounded forward and back, herding us along. We walked to the end of the dirt road and snooped around looking for the old jeep trail. It was unmistakable on the map, but there was no sign of it now. Instead, clumps of green and yellow grasses swayed in the breeze. We followed a parting in the grasses to a patch of raspberry brambles. It became clear that we were tracking a herd path. It seemed to be going toward the mountain base so we continued. The patch of brambles gradually spread into a wide field, the thorns growing sharper and the bushes higher as we advanced. The forest that once stood here had been stolen many years before. So nature sowed brambles of the meanest sort, a vengeful warning to stay away. The shrubs were now chin high and we could not see our boots. We had been hiking for two hours and had gone barely a mile.

"What do you think, Jane?" I asked, my frustration growing. "Should we keep going?"

"I don't know. I have a long drive home to Albany this evening. Maybe we'd better turn back."

Strangely, the reverse herd path didn't seem as straight as the original route. And then I spotted something in a tree about thirty feet ahead. Built into a tree, twelve feet above the ground, was a wooden platform. It had four plywood walls with small slats in two of the walls. A hunter's blind. I imagined the brambles being visited by a doe happily chewing the buds, unaware that any moment her life could be ended by some inexplicable force aiming at her from above. And now we were in the brambles. Was someone watching us?

* * *

It was clear that we were not re-tracing our original steps. Somehow we had ended up on a parallel herd path.

"Wendy, hold up a minute, let me pull out my map and compass."

"Sure," I replied, trying to mask my fear of being lost on this hidden mountain.

Jane pointed at the map. "Look. If we follow a straight compass bearing from where we thought we were to where we think we should be going, we should find our way back to the dirt road."

What Jane said made sense, although I couldn't explain why. I trusted her and she led us back to the road. Our first attempt at climbing Lookout had failed. We walked back to the house, a bit dejected but already planning our next attempt.

The next summer we sat on my porch planning Attempt Number Two.

"I think where we started from last time was too northerly," I said, pointing at the map. "We might find this old jeep trail if we begin from a different corner of the dirt road."

Jane looked at Mollie and stroked her furry head, "What do you think Mollie-girl? Should we try this route?"

By her excited leaps, I guessed Mollie could tell we were about to go for a romp in the woods. And so we started off again. Northeast of the dirt road we crossed a creek and moved into the woods, this time following only compass bearings. The forest here was immature, a thick mix of brambles and young hardwoods and softwoods. After an hour or so, we began to ascend. As we climbed higher, the woods thinned, but so did our daylight. An hour and a half later, we reached the top of a shoulder in the mountain. Looking south, we could see the summit taunting us. The true peak was a couple of miles and at least an hour of bushwhacking away. But we didn't have enough daylight to complete the hike. We would have to return home.

Twice thwarted, I felt more determined than ever to reach the peak and learn its secrets. I wonder now how Jane felt about trying again. We had always hiked a variety of mountains every summer and I was compelling her to share my Lookout mission. I felt the pressure of time. Time makes almost no difference to a mountain, yet completely shapes a person's life. Did Jane care about scaling this mountain as much as I did? Was one trail as vital to her as any other? She never said.

* * *

On September 8, 1995, Jane, Mollie, and I met again and strategized. The days were shorter, so we had to choose correctly. The topo map showed a double track that looped toward the base of the mountain about a half-mile south from where we had started the last time. We found the beginning of the double track, and to our surprise, it appeared to be used regularly. We continued an easy walk along it, with nothing more than high grass and goldenrods tickling our knees. As we progressed, it became clear why this trail was so worn. It was a dumping ground for old appliances, car parts, and patio furniture. The farther we progressed, the older the junk was. We vowed one day to return with a wheelbarrow to reclaim an old Adirondack love seat that lay with its memories among the refuse. We never did.

After an hour or so of hiking, the path became confusing. Orange tape tied to branches formed a straight line through the trees. Crisscrossing this line like a large X was another swath marked with blue survey tape. Loggers, I thought. It was impossible to distinguish the jeep trail from the survey cuts. Jane checked the map. "It looks like the old trail may turn north here. Have a good look around and memorize some landmarks for the trip back."

I counted the dead limbs on a nearby paper birch. Mollie circled around, sniffing. Then I looked in the direction of the summit and silently asked The Mountain for permission to ascend. We continued along the trail until we got close to the base. From there, we determined the compass bearing that should take us to the summit. At the point where we left the trail to bushwhack through the forest, I tied a sweatshirt around a tree. The way was thick at first, and we had to pull apart old fir limbs to move forward. But as we ascended, the forest thinned, as if granting us grace. We continued for about an hour, climbing higher than the loggers and their chainsaws. The forest smelled of humus, the ground felt soft and sacred underfoot. Eventually the grade became so steep it was necessary to grab onto saplings to pull ahead and keep from sliding back. We climbed at what felt like a 60-degree angle, using our hands and legs, our heads inches from the ground. Being taller than Jane I was able to climb farther and got ahead of her and Mollie. They were no longer in sight. I was alone on The Mountain. I stopped to wait for them and looked up toward the sky. An enormous rock face loomed above me. The cool forest had given way to the warmth of a stone atrium at least twenty yards wide. My heart pounded as I realized that this was the rocky crag that had teased and beckoned me over the years from miles away. I felt like a young child who had just discovered something new about the world. But the something new I had discovered was ancient. My legs began to fly forward, with Jane and Mollie tracing my route.

"We're here! We've made it!" I shouted, my voice cracking in excitement. The rock face was steeper than I had imagined, too steep to scramble up. Our only choice was to skirt the ridge and use the bordering trees as levers. We hoisted ourselves onto the top of the rock face. It was warm and peaceful. Jane, Mollie, and I stood upon the summit of Lookout Mountain. Below us, we could see Loon Lake and the cottages dotting its shoreline.

So this is what God sees.

We sat down and ate our food. I pressed the rough surface of the warm rock into my fingers. I recognized the steep red roof of our summer house far below. For some reason, it surprised me that I could not see through the kitchen window.

After some time, Jane, Mollie, and I began our descent. We followed our reverse compass bearings carefully, testing our skills against Mollie's nose. We made it to the old trail only twenty feet from where we had entered the forest, marked by my sweatshirt (Mollie was right on the mark). Excited, we moved quickly along the old trail, chatting and laughing. And suddenly the trail ended. More precisely, it went off in four different directions.

"We're back at the area of surveying. Look at all these paths going off into the woods! Do you remember which way we came from?" I asked, hoping Jane had kept better track of our route than I had.

"No, I don't. Let me follow this blue-taped path for a bit. It seems like it should be heading back in the right direction."

"OK, but don't go too far."

I was alone again. The Mountain wasn't through with us yet.

Jane returned after about ten minutes. "This trail's no good. It only takes me deeper into the woods."

As Jane and I talked about what to do, we noticed Mollie move through some trees.

"Mollie, come back, girl," Jane called, afraid of losing her.

Mollie returned but as Jane and I talked, she went back to the same trees. We called her back again and once again let her go. This time we followed. Mollie led us straight out of the forest and back onto the old double-track trail.

I have never forgotten that trip up Lookout, the challenges of finding our way, the encounters with unseen loggers and hunters and the humility that was required before we were granted access to the peak. The journey was one that I could have shared only with Jane.

Thirteen years later, in the summer of 2008, I decided to hike up Lookout again. It was the year after Jane's death. Jane had been forty-six, in the summer of her life, when she was diagnosed with stage IV lung cancer. Jane never smoked—you couldn't find a pair of lungs that had breathed more clean Adirondack air than Jane's. She died three months later. I needed answers. And I needed to get those answers in a place where I would feel closer to where she was.

I had heard that a trail had been marked all the way to the top. The route was different from the one that Jane, Mollie, and I had taken. All those years ago, we had bushwhacked to the summit. And although we tried to follow a trail that seemed to be stitched as permanently as the mountain drawn on the map, the steps we took were singular and never lasting. The ice storm of 1998 had made that route impenetrable, reclaiming it forever. And now here was this easy trail to the top. It had been blazed by the local hunting club, which had leased the land from the timber company. The Mountain had found a way to harness those forces that had stolen life from it and created such daunting obstacles for Jane and me. And now those same forces were allowing me to get back to the mountaintop and find a route back to her.

Coping with a sudden and inexplicable death is a trail-less mountain peak. There is no path, no accurate topographical map to guide you. The only compass point is your heart. In the weeks after her death, Jane's family came to visit me. We stood together on my dock on Loon Lake within sight of Lookout Mountain and poured out some of Jane's ashes. The soft gray specks scattered into the sparkling waters and caught on the breeze. Here Jane would rest, her physical body joining the plankton and the lake trout that live in the waters and the jewelweed that grows along the shore. Her spirit is now a permanent part of this place. And my friendship with her will stay as eternal as The Mountain. *you don't mention Mollie*

Where the Trail Ends

14

Catching a Fish

* * *

LEAH TITCOMB

2012

I stood on the shore in a cloud of no-see-ums, tiny bugs that would make me swell and burn until I got away from them and managed to stop itching. As long as I stood on the shore, it wouldn't be getting any better. I hustled to get my girls to tie down their stuff in the canoes and push off into the moving stream, away from the bugs. When we finally launched our boats, I was able to stop scratching my bites and focus more intentionally on instructing my students. Some were more frustrated than others.

I dipped my paddle into the Penobscot River and pulled the canoe forward. It silently arced through the current, propelling me into the interconnecting waterways of Maine. The teenage girl in my bow looked intently at her paddle as if she could will it to make us go in the direction she wanted. It was the first time she had ever canoed, despite having grown up in Maine, where the waterways run endlessly between Canada and the coast.

The other Old Town canoes wove around us, each girl with a determined and slightly strained look as she dipped her paddle in the water and tried to steer her canoe. After a few minutes of concentrated silence, the girls started giggling and bumping into each other and the riverbank. Their voices rang out, shrill directions for the bow- or stern-woman on how to make the canoe move the way they wanted it to.

Chelsea was in my bow, and she watched her paddle move

through the water, experimenting with different strokes. Pry. Draw. Pry. Our canoe wobbled with each of her strokes, and I kept correcting its path.

We paddled noisily away from Lobster Trip Boat Launch, our last sign of civilization for the next 170 miles. The trees on the riverbank engulfed us, and the girls' voices reverberated through the tall pines, chasing away every moose, rabbit, and chipmunk within miles. Fish slipped beneath rocks at our approach.

No surprise

Canoe Expeditions for Maine Girls offered a chance to connect with a wild and scenic part of the state. These girls had applied and been accepted to the program, and now I was guiding them on a scholarship-funded, three-week paddling expedition. I could tell they were all wondering what they had gotten themselves into as they let the river pull them into the wilderness. They kept looking back over their shoulders, then at each other with wide eyes, joking about the horror films that started this way.

right

* * *

We made camp our first night at the same primitive campsite where Henry David Thoreau had slept in the mid-1800s, and where my grandparents had stayed in 1941 on their own north woods canoe trip. This was familiar territory for me. I held the ax handle, smooth and cool in my hands, and demonstrated how to split wood for our evening fire. The swarms of blackflies and mosquitoes would die down with the smoke, and the girls assigned to fire building quickly took charge.

Just as in the time of Thoreau and his companions, every person is essential to running a smooth camp. Once the girls had learned their tasks, the only sound was the high-pitched whirr of the Coleman stove, the squeak of the water pump, the snapping of twigs, and the thump of the ax against logs. I didn't need to nag anyone to do her chores because it was immediately and readily apparent that we depended on one another for warmth, food, and safety. The girls wanted to be comfortable and, for that to be possible, they all had to pitch in. I could tell that the girls took pride in their work; they obviously felt valued and useful as they learned the basic skills it took to live in the woods. They couldn't open the refrigerator here, close the door on the mosquitoes, or run the tap water. They were starting to understand what it really meant to eat, drink, and be warm.

Delia hovered over the green camp stove, holding the metal spatula uncertainly as the onions sizzled in the pan. She looked at me. She opened her mouth, closed it, and then opened it again, as if to say something.

"What is it, Delia?"

"I've never sautéed onions before."

I smiled. "Now you have. Keep moving them around so they don't burn."

The next morning I awoke early and sat at the river's edge with my grandfather's small leather-bound journal in my lap and my fly rod next to me. I opened the creased binding, its pliable leather softly flopping open. He and Granny had stayed here, loaded with provisions for the journey. The tall dark pines that he wrote about were now emerging from the mist in front of me. I sat on the river's edge sipping my tea.

Everything was still and silent, except for the rush of the water. This was one of my favorite times of day. It was my time with the land. I waded out into the shallow water with my rod and cast a few loops.

This is a secret part of the Northeast, rarely talked about or ravaged by hordes of tourists because it is too remote for most people. It is solitary and isolated; the trees stand undisturbed by loggers. I reeled in my line and called the girls to join me by the riverside and appreciate the free-flowing water.

They gathered around me, sleepy-eyed and groggy. When their eyes started to focus more, I had them visualize the river, not as it was now, but packed with rolling logs, tumbling over the rocks from bank to bank, like a box of cigars. The river was part of their heritage and mine.

Once, the water was full of floating logs being driven to sawmills on the coast, and before that, the rivers were highways for trappers and Indians. Loggers' voices and the sound of their saws cutting pine trees used to fill the woods. The loggers drove the pine logs through rapids and over waterfalls, living in makeshift camps from here to Canada.

To get the trees to the mills, loggers would roll the trees into the rivers, and the trees would float, packed tightly and bumping against the banks and rocks. The loggers would run across the logs, standing on the rolling mass as it moved through the water, breaking up logjams and herding the logs, trying not to catch a foot or roll under the logs.

Now this waterway is a quiet road into deeper wilderness. It leads to the Allagash River, the only river in Maine that is designated a federal wild and scenic river. Only two old dams block its flow and the passage of fish. In most places, it looks the same as when Thoreau canoed it, and the French-Canadian trappers before him, and the Native Americans before them.

The waterway is still set in a working forest, but logs don't travel to market on the river anymore. Fortunately, the sounds of trucks and chainsaws don't penetrate the silence too often. The land around the corridor is mostly untouched for miles, and the only things downriver are fish and sporadic canoes.

The farther we canoed down the Allagash, the more sunken logs we would float over, their bark eerily preserved in the cold water. The girls would start shouting out when they found more, trapped between rocks, or half buried in mud.

Some logs would have thick spikes still driven into their sides, with dark rust sliding off and tainting the girls' hands as they reached to touch a piece of the past. The logs and spikes wouldn't be a problem in the slower-moving water but, in the rapids, I would have to keep my eyes peeled as I steered the canoe through mounds of whitewater.

For now, standing on the smooth ledges of Gero Island, I concentrated on the maps spread out before me and drew our watery course through rivers and ponds with my pencil. In some places, we were going to have to go short distances upstream to reach the next body of water. Some of the girls crowded around me, their faces close to mine, strands of stringy hair dangling down like tendrils. We squatted around the maps, pointing to different sections, rapids, and historical places. They were very concerned about going upriver for eight miles. I grinned and told them to imagine that they were fish fighting their way up the river from the ocean.

* * *

Some of them glanced at my fishing rod leaning against the dark green hull of my canoe, and one tentatively pointed out that I hadn't caught anything. "That's because we haven't gotten to the good spots yet," I said. This waterway has been the traditional route of countless salmon, trout, river herring, and alewives. Their numbers have been reduced with the construction of dams on Maine's waterways, but the Allagash has fish ladders on its dams, increasing the chance of survival.

A fish ladder is essentially a series of steps with water flowing over them, allowing the fish to jump from pool to pool, around or over a dam, as if it were a navigable waterfall. Fish ladders have been partially successful in helping to restore fish populations. For some fish, a ladder can provide a huge victory, but they haven't helped others. Each species can only jump a certain distance and height, so making a ladder that accommodates all species is very difficult.

The abundance of dams on Maine rivers, particularly the Penobscot and the Kennebec, prevent fish and eel populations from traveling between feeding and spawning areas. The concrete walls, some up to 100 feet high, typically store water to generate electric power. When moving downriver, fish often get caught and killed in the thrashing blades of the turbines.

The Atlantic Salmon Commission counts the number of fish that return to Maine to spawn each year. In the early 1800s, hundreds of thousands of salmon spawned in the rivers of northeast Maine. In 2010, fewer then two thousand returned.

There have been thousands of dams in Maine history. Most of the early ones provided power for sawmills, then for textile mills. The river drivers sometimes used dams to stop or divert the flow of logs along the waterways. Dams also trapped water to power paper and pulp mills. Now the water flowing over most of Maine's dams generates electricity. We produce so much electricity that Maine actually sells the excess to Massachusetts and Connecticut.

The dams littering Maine's waterways are not all in use. Some hydroelectric dams have been recently taken out of service, others have been abandoned for decades, with no known purpose. For the most part, these abandoned dams remain in the river, blocking the passage of fish to their spawning grounds.

* * *

The next morning, I again stood on the banks of the river alone. I cast my line, watching my forward loop unfurl over the current. The fly skimmed the river surface before delicately landing. Because the free-flowing water moved it too quickly, I cast again, hitting the eddy line, so the fish could get a better look at it. I let the fly float slowly along the eddy, waiting for a fish to bite.

Several casts later, I reeled in my line, tucked my rod into the canoe, and paddled to a new spot along the river. I knew there were fish out there, but I wasn't sure what kind or how many. As the river narrowed, I floated up to some odd muck sticking out of the current. As I got closer, I realized it was a pile of old logs and cement blocks, covered with shreds of canvas. It was an old canvas dam, stretching the span of the river, the shreds of cloth bobbing eerily just under the surface. I carefully picked my way through the mess, trying not to get caught in it, wondering if there were many fish beyond the dam.

Rivers and fish can recover if they are given the chance. Many activists have called for the removal of dams along major rivers and the addition of fish passages to those that remain. But the destruction of dams is controversial. Hydroelectricity is "clean" power; it doesn't require the burning of fossil fuels. But if a hydroelectric dam doesn't have a fish ladder, it can cause other environmental and economic problems.

I gripped my rod and cast my line, hoping the fish here had had time to make a comeback—hoping to catch a glimpse of one on the end of my line. I sent my line out in careful and swift loops, making the fly dance through the air. The rod became an extension of my forearm, and I moved it back and forth in slow motion, making sure the line didn't tangle as the fly made low figure-eights over the river. Fly-fishing is meditative time with the river. I had not brought my rod on the trip to provide food, but to practice an art and get to know the river more intimately. *good thing*

* * *

My connection with the land is through the water, through my family's history in northern Maine and along the coast. I was passionate about showing one of my favorite rivers to this group of Maine girls. Instead of texting or Facebooking, they stood around me, knee-deep in the cold current, learning to cast a fly rod, to recognize where a fish might be, to mimic a bug landing on the water.

I handed the rod to Judy and stood next to her, holding her arm, helping her to get the feel of casting. She smiled and concentrated on the motion and the water. The other girls stood to one side of me and watched Judy. I pointed to where the water was flowing fast, then to where it slowed down, and explained how the fish used the current to their advantage, just as we did in the canoes. I explained how fish can take a break in the eddies, not using any more energy than they have to. If a fly is in a place where the fish would have to expend more energy to catch it than it would gain by eating it, the fish will typically watch it float by. Judy cast on her own, laughing when the line tangled, then trying again to get the fly to the right spot.

Jocelyn wanted to try next. She had been fishing with her uncle, but hadn't been able to cast; he had done most of the casting while she had hung out. I let her hold the rod and gripped her forearm, just as I had with Judy. Jocelyn's face squished up in concentration as she threw the fly-line out toward the eddy. I let go of her arm and let her cast on her own.

As Jocelyn was casting, I turned to the other girls and made sure they understood the importance of using the current to our advantage, both when fishing and canoeing. Using the current was symbolic of the way we traveled in the wilderness: "going with the flow," adapting to changing weather and situations. Like fish, we could use currents to help us move without overexerting ourselves.

We depend on the river—it can teach us many things. The girls watched the fly move and learned how fish use the current. They learned how to maneuver their canoes without fighting the flow. They also were discovering the history of their state and taking pride in it. These waterways are ancient. The sunken logs and spikes were reminders of their ancestors. The river's water carried our canoes over the same rocks and past the same banks as those of the Native Americans and fur traders.

Meanwhile, the grueling portages kept the waterway private and gave the girls a sense of pride in their passage to the wilderness. They would learn their strength as women, mentally and physically, by paddling more than 170 miles and portaging their 80-pound canoes for two-mile stretches. In an age when teenagers are bombarded with messages about how they should look and act, these girls would get the chance to redefine themselves without outside pressures. They would be challenged to be strong, and would have female role models to help them realize that strength. After seeing a woman fish competently, Jocelyn got the chance to feel that she also could learn to fish competently. She was trying it herself, instead of passively watching.

These girls' connection with the river would only strengthen as they learned more about its history, how to fish the water, and how to guide canoes through the rapids. They were learning to fish in the same river that Thoreau and my grandfather (and his father before him) had fished. The girls were excited both by the experience of casting and the idea of trying to predict where a fish might be. Each girl took a turn with the rod while others cheered the caster on and pointed to where they thought the most fish would be hiding.

While staying at the same primitive campsites that Thoreau wrote so eloquently about, we talked about the fact that women also can explore the wilderness. These girls were experiencing the Allagash much as it had been more than one hundred years ago, and much as it will be for the next hundred years—if young people like them continue to support the Wild and Scenic Rivers Act of 1968. If these girls help to keep the river wild, their own daughters might also learn their own strengths while experiencing the independence of traveling by canoe.

The Allagash is the last wild river in the east. Other rivers in Maine, such as the Penobscot and Kennebec, might have more visibility or volume, but they also are more developed. Hydroelectric dams trap the fish and clutter the waterways. Roads run next to them, and bridges span their width.

The Allagash originally had only two access points, but that number has been increasing due to pressure from special interests. We accessed it in the traditional way, via the chain of rivers and lakes stemming from the Penobscot River. If there hadn't been so many dams interrupting the Penobscot, we could have canoed almost the entire length of Maine. Instead, we drove to a point where the river was free-flowing, and we could paddle unencumbered to the Allagash.

Standing in the current, the girls felt the power of the water pushing against their legs. They joked about how strong their legs had become, and how their paddling arms could defeat any obstacle. It was heartwarming to hear them talk so confidently about their bodies and their abilities after hearing their doubts earlier in the trip. It made me smile to hear them talking passionately about fish and asking questions about waterway rights and politics. Delia handed the rod back to me after her turn, and I made sure everyone had had her fill of casting before I took the rod and looked out over the river.

The glistening side of a fish flickered for a split-second beneath the water. I cast the fly to where I had seen the flash. The tops of trout are dark, with vermicular patterns that blend in with the dark river bottom. The undersides are silvery, to blend in with the lighter sky. Holding my breath, shoulders tense and ready, I let the fly float, then tugged it a few times to mimic a struggling fly on the water. The end of my rod dipped slightly, and with a small flick of my wrist, I set the hook into the fish's lip. I reeled in against the strain of the struggling fish. After the fish wore itself out, I dipped my net into the water and brought it briefly ashore. The fish gasped, moving its thick-lipped mouth as if it were trying to speak to us. The silvery scales on its sides, like tiny mirrors, reflected light back at the marveling girls. When everyone had had a chance to see her, and before she ran out of oxygen in her gills, I put her back into the water, holding her gently until she regained enough strength to slide out of my cupped hands and dash away with the flick of her dark tail.

We stood in the river. Silently. Smiling. Listening to the sound of free-flowing water.

15

Epigoni, Revisited

* * *

MICHAEL WEJCHERT

2013, Winner

> The machine does not isolate man from the great problems
> of nature but plunges him more deeply into them.
>
> ANTOINE DE SAINT-EXUPÉRY

 We are not in New England. Certainly. Caribou tracks end in small dots beneath Paul Roderick's single-engine DHC-2 Beaver. Denali, where Paul knows glacial landings like city slickers know commuter shortcuts, is not much more than a hundred miles away. Every once in a while, Paul lets go of the rudder to take a picture, and the plane bucks wildly. Opening the window, offering his camera to the polar air, he snaps photos of mountains without names. Bayard Russell, Elliot Gaddy, and I have all flown with Paul before, but we've never seen him like this. We exchange nervous glances.

When we cornered Paul a few days ago in the small town of Talkeetna, Alaska, he was incredulous. "You want me to land *where?*"

I bluff. "Rob Wing from Fairbanks has landed there tons of times, Paul."

"Wing says he's landed everywhere." He scoffs, but it works. Pilots are like climbers. The spark of competition, adventure, is usually all you need to light a fire.

"All right. Get me a map and I might be able to get you boys in there."

Bayard, Elliot, and I clink glasses at the bar a few minutes later.

We're going to Mount Deborah.

Alpinist magazine released the news in February. "The Copp-Dash Inspire Award announced the 2013 winners of the climbing grant established in memory of American climbers Jonny Copp and Micah Dash, who were killed in an avalanche in China, along with filmmaker Wade Johnson. In addition to providing financial support to prospective expedition teams, the goal of the Copp-Dash Inspire Award is to . . . help the climbers bring back and share inspiring multimedia stories of their adventures." And there our scruffy names were, in print. Shaking, I phoned my parents.

"We're going. We got the money. I need to buy a nice camera."

There was a silence. My parents remember Copp, Dash, and Johnson's deaths well. In 2009, the climbers were in China while I scaled mountains on my first Alaskan expedition. Standing vigil by the phone, my parents had been jarred by the news of their deaths. That spring moment, as Paul landed with our own, live, sunburned, emaciated bodies, the moment my mother heard my voice on a regular, non-satellite telephone, must have allowed them to exhale.

Paul actually points out Mount Deborah's unclimbed south face as the plane slices through the freezing air, although it is not difficult to find. It stands out, to say the least. A shriek of granite churned upward by some massive thrust, sentinel, alone. Unlike the jagged "teeth" of the Central Alaska Range, whose steep walls form a phalanx of igneous molars, Deborah heaves upward sistered by nothing: a rotting fang in an otherwise empty mouth. The mountain is terrifying: one of the most dangerous in North America, miles from anywhere, swathed in snow.

"There's the road, if you need to walk out," Paul says into his headset.

I toss a glance at Bayard, sitting in the seat next to me, ten years my senior. Though he can't whisper discreetly over the thrum of the engine, I can tell he's never heard Paul say *that* before, either. We can barely make out the snowy Denali Highway, a good forty miles from our mountain.

In 1964, David Roberts and Don Jensen hiked this distance on a failed attempt at Deborah, only to limp out forty-two days later, disappointed but grateful to get out alive. It was Roberts's book, *Deborah: A Wilderness Narrative* (Vanguard Press, 1970), written in terse, uncompromising prose, which convinced me to come here, though as a daydreaming eighth-grader, I might have underestimated the severity of Alaskan climbing.

* * *

"Are you bringing a satellite phone?" David asks. We're in Cambridge, Massachusetts, days before our trip. I've just spent more money on parking than I do for a week of food, and the eighth-grader in me can't believe I'm hashing out logistics with the legendary David Roberts, who pokes at a salad. No one in the restaurant would guess Roberts was at one time a famous Alaskan explorer, but then again, they aren't close enough to see his eyes, which flare with passion as the discussion dives into crevasses, hovers over safe bivouac spots, or rests on the technical difficulties of climbing in the cold.

When Roberts and Jensen tried Mount Deborah in 1964, their two-way radio broke down early and they had no communication with the outside world. For day after forlorn day, the pair sat in isolation, whiling away their hours, thwarted by an unyielding mountain and each other's psyches.

I wonder how Dave feels about us making a film, which is our plan. Is it sacrilege? Years ago, when Talkeetna was a tiny spot on the map, when Dave and a few others made tentative prods into the stunning peaks of the Alaska range, mountaineering wasn't so much of a commodity.

For my part, I feel as if our plan, involving thousands of dollars of borrowed camera equipment, promised pictures to various sponsors, the inevitable trip report and Facebook updates, and above all, a 248-mile flight, is preposterous and unfair to the mountain.

Part of this stems from an impassioned letter Dave penned to Alpinist magazine in 2007. "It hit me that the young climbers of the day were what the Greeks called *epigoni*: the born-too-late, the hangers on." The letter stopped me in my nascent tracks. "There are still, to be sure, magnificent challenges left for climbers . . . but . . . nearly all the hardest mountains in the world have been climbed." Going to Dave's mountain, to the place that had sprouted a title with the words "a wilderness narrative," in Paul's shiny new aircraft with our solar chargers and iPods—were we hammering the nail in the coffin?

Had technology finally tripped over adventure?

According to Facebook, seventy-six people "like" the fact that we're heading to Mount Deborah. As the plane leaves the tarmac, Bayard's iPhone loses service and we stop sending photos of ourselves to his wife Anne, who has been posting them. Accurate weather forecasting, satellite phone updates, and Paul's prodigal ability to coax an aircraft into locations other pilots cannot—all these have warped one of the most remote places on earth into a playground for alpine climbers. This paradigm shift convinced the three of us to unearth an obscure objective such as Deborah, where we would almost certainly not see another soul.

The irony is not lost on me that, to finance our monkish stint of isolation, we've ended up promising footage, photographs, and words to our sponsors. By our doing so, Deborah becomes a little less legendary with each click of the shutter.

* * *

None of that is running through my head just now. If writers ever state they are thinking such delicate thoughts in the mountains, they're liars: they're just horrified, like the rest of us. At the moment, I am not wondering if our impact on Mount Deborah is valid:

Epigoni, Revisited

Elliot has just skied into a crevasse and he might be hurt or dead. There aren't any blog posts in this world, just Bayard and I trying to dig an anchor in deep snow, praying that one of our best friends is alive.

When we landed two days ago, the south face of Mount Deborah took our breath away. In forty collective years of climbing experience, we'd never seen anything like it. From the air, we could feign aloofness, but as Paul flew away, stranding us on the West Fork Glacier, we felt vulnerable.

Sweat tinged my back despite the cold. We were utterly alone in one of the wildest places on earth. When we intruders stood still, nothing moved. No animal lived. No raven's wings made silent brushstrokes against the shockingly blue sky. Four miles up the glacier, past all the sleeping crevasses, past all the avalanche-soaked passes, lay the apex of years of dreams—and nightmares.

This place could kill us instantly if it wanted to. I think of Copp, Dash, and Johnson. Did they have time to turn the camera off before the avalanche rang its final note?

After half an hour or so, Elliot emerges again. My friend is fine. His sunglasses have fallen off and his skis dangle below him. Skiing back over crevasse fields is indescribable: an odd mixture of boredom and constant, nagging fear. Flat, uninteresting terrain cloaks the menacing possibility of breaking through to the world's underbelly. As we return to base camp, all of us cringe, waiting for another plunge.

*　*　*

"Why do you need to go to Mount Deborah?" The question is simple, but grating. I am streaking across Vermont in my Toyota Corolla with my friend Anna. We have just come back from a hike, one we've both done dozens of times, though each time is different, and crystalline in my mind: new snow on scraggly cedars, a resilient hobblebush, a slow pace, our nostrils stinging from cold on the summit.

"It's *new*. It's unexplored. It's *mystery*."

"Why isn't this enough? Why aren't these moments significant for you?"

I offer my best response: that to find adventure in wild places these days, you've got to construct your own, that to keep pace with helicopters and cell phones and idiot-proof GPS devices, you've got to burrow further, create challenges, go to mountains without names. I neglect to mention, of course, that we will rely on all of these things on our trip to some extent.

But these moments at home *are* enough. Sometimes. I remember completing a hut-to-hut traverse in the White Mountains with my friend Tristan, our feet pounding fifty-two miles of New Hampshire schist and granite, naked save running shoes and shorts. The summer's heat, and the route's closeness to buildings and people, had allowed us to take no possessions or food. Deborah offers no such choice.

"Isn't it contrived? Or selfish? To fly in to a place like that?"

For this I have no real answer. The farther north I get from the trappings of the digital age, the more of them I seem to carry in my bag.

* * *

Not long after we've arrived, I stop worrying about contrivance, or about being fair to Mount Deborah. It's clear that although we have planes and satellite phones in our quiver, the mountain can still surprise us.

Polar air, a freak occurrence even for April in Alaska, settles over base camp, and we begin to freeze. Everything—hand sanitizer, meat, bagels, contact lens solution—becomes a solid block. We will find out afterward it is Alaska's coldest spring since 1923.

"I've never been so goddamn cold in my life," says Bayard flatly. Bayard, at thirty-six, is one of the best winter climbers in the United States. I had a picture of him on my wall long before I met him.

When I first moved to New Hampshire, I was too nervous to talk to him. I've seen Bayard laugh off thirty-foot falls, wend his way up serpentine cracks chocked with ice, defy physics. The clothing company Outdoor Research is paying for him to be here, and he adds an air of legitimacy to Elliot's and my youthful, angst-ridden drive.

The snow squeaks when our skis touch it. In the silence, the sound is almost deafening. We keep our cameras tucked inside our shirts, even at night, and I live with the battery for the satellite phone in my pants pocket. Our plan is to climb Deborah with day packs and a single stove, in a push, descend over the other side, and trudge back to base camp. This requires perfect weather, total confidence in our abilities, and the complete willingness to live in unspeakable danger for three or more days.

"Michael. This isn't going to work." Bayard and I are talking, the day before we have decided to launch. I try not to think of my parents, a world away. "We'll freeze our toes. Best case scenario. No question."

After a sleepless night, we awake at 4:00 in the morning, the three of us chattering as we melt water in the tent. It is 40 below zero here, at 5,000 feet. What will happen when we climb higher? I force myself out of the tent and stumble around, shouting at the violent cold.

"C'mon DEBORAH!" I scream, a jilted lover. "Let us CLIMB!"

Our systems have failed us. I do not snap photographs; exposed skin means frostbite. After everyone wakes up, we ski toward the wall in our down jackets. Our feet, buried in neoprene-lined double boots, are without feeling. For a second I am detached. I start weighing how many toes I am willing to lose before I turn around. For a minute, I contemplate this perverse absurdity in the arctic dawn. The rope between the three of us suddenly comes tight. Bayard, stopping, forty-five minutes away from base camp. The virgin face looms above us still.

"I'm going back. I strongly suggest you guys do the same."

Our plans are unraveling. By now, success seems impossible. But just a few minutes of footage, Elliot and I climbing on the face . . . *something* for the grant committee. I take some rope from Bayard. Elliot takes some climbing gear. We keep going. *Is this what Jonny and Micah thought as they pushed forward with Wade? Or Dave and Don? Does the camera make us any less vulnerable?*

I realize the mountain doesn't care who we are, why we're here, or what we've brought. My frozen fingers unzip four layers and finally fumble with the camera lens. I manage thirty seconds of shaky footage almost automatically: Elliot below the mountain, swinging his feet like a football punter to stay warm. I don't need the film to remember the moment though: we two grown men doing jumping jacks, miles from anywhere, beneath a hunk of granite no one really cares about, pistons of humanity bobbing up and down, fighting for enough warmth to stay alive. The climbing ceases to matter, and the movie, too. Sometimes, surviving is enough.

After fifteen minutes of this, we clip into our skis, still intent. I cannot feel my feet. "Elliot."

"Yo!"

"I'm calling it."

"Yeah?"

"Yeah. This is suicide."

A pause.

"Yup."

In the end, it's that easy.

Bayard clasps our disappointed shoulders. He hustles me into my sleeping bag and hands hot-water bottles to shove next to my feet. Six hours later, all our gear packed, we hear the thrum of Paul's Beaver, stabbing through two weeks of silence. The bright red and blue of the plane's fuselage against a clear sky, against the white of Alaska. For a moment, everything fits, as Paul lands to pick up his grateful *epigoni*.

16

Steward's Story

* * *

DEVON REYNOLDS

2013, Runner-up

Technology sometimes seems to run the world. The dinging noises and flashing icons have urgency to them that compels communication at an ever-quickening pace. I need my cell phone to find my family picking me up at the airport. I need my e-mail in case a professor sends me some new information right before class. I get stuck in the mentality that I will lose touch: with the world and, more important, with my friends. My generation, the Millennials, functions with a rapidity that threatens to overwhelm even high-powered computers. We schedule our days down to the minute, sometimes so closely that we don't realize we've overbooked. I can't count the times a friend has texted me just before we were supposed to meet up, asking for a rain check. I am also guilty of such errors, but I imagine I regret them more than my peers because I have known the value of a different form of communication, and community.

Six sleepy bodies crowd around the staff dining table at the Adirondack Loj outside of Lake Placid. We're the 2011 Adirondack High Peaks Summit Stewards, bent over bowls of cereal and plates of Bisquick pancakes, wolfing down calories to sustain our strained existence. We take our turns telling the stories of the last two weeks; we ask the questions we've been storing up; we lay plans for the days to come. It has been half a month since we have all been together, but we laugh and groan together, a close-knit group.

When the staff meeting ends, Julia heads up to the office to attend to administrative duties as chief and commander of the crew. Gina retraces the short walk from the main Loj building to the dilapidated yurt where we live on our days off, and climbs back into bed to enjoy her day of rest. The rest of us hoist our packs for another hike. Sam gets into her car to drive to the trailhead for Cascade Mountain, a short, steep hike off the highway twenty minutes from the Loj. The other three of us start down the old Marcy Dam trail, shrunk into a foot-wide path by its twenty-year retirement from frequent foot traffic. A quarter of a mile in, Libby heads off along the seven-mile track to Mount Marcy while Zack and I turn aside. The two of us hike together for three miles, talking when we're not panting, until our trails, too, split. I hike toward Wright Peak where, just at treeline, I stop to watch the slide on Algonquin Peak, a large patch of exposed rock clearly visible across a ravine on the side of the mountain. I can see Zack's tan clothes and blue pack ascend the slide. When he disappears into the trees again, I turn back to my own summit and head up for another day of work.

Five days a week, for three months, I worked for eight hours a day on top of one mountain or another in the Adirondacks, working to protect rare alpine vegetation that survives on only 100 acres of land in New York State. Wherever I stood, I knew that on the other four peaks stood four other stewards: my doppelgängers swathed in sweat-stained khaki with the summit steward badge sewn on to make uniforms. I knew they were there from the voices I heard on the radio when they signed in and out each morning and night, and from the mud-stained schedule I carried.

We lived a shared and solitary life. We hiked the same trails and slept in the same tents. We borrowed recipes from one another. We talked about the peaks as if they were rooms in a house, our house, so familiar we could grope our way around them even with the lights off. We all looked for the brain-shaped rock near the

Algonquin summit to reassure us that we had almost finished hiking. We all hid from the rain in the same coffin-sized space under a rock on Cascade. We all did these things, but we did them alone. One steward per peak. Staggered days off. Rotated peak assignments. And during the workweek, we each camped by ourselves, a few miles below the various peaks. I read two or three books a week and still slept twelve hours a night. Zack got lonely and hiked out to the Loj as often as possible. Sam couldn't sleep because of that trapped feeling, which we all felt at times during the summer, of being alone in the woods with only a nylon tent between her and the unknown.

Without cell-phone reception or computers, we had little contact during our days on duty. Humans are social creatures, however, so we found ways to stay in touch. We waved to one another each day from our peaks, though the distance made it impossible to see the gesture. It was enough for us to know that our friends, however invisible, were remembering us when they looked across the miles of mountainous landscape. When we met hikers who were summiting two peaks, we asked them to deliver messages to each other. We left notes on each other's beds in the yurt. These tiny tokens bore us through the isolation of our work, allowed us to commune despite separation. Most important, we lined the trails with stories for one another.

First Telling

Well, I met a naked hiker this week.

(*General astonishment, questioning.*)

Oh, yes, completely naked. I thought at first that he had some
   shorts on . . . but when I got closer I realized, no, no, he had it
   all hanging out.

(*Shock, humor, questioning.*)

I told him he might want to put some clothes on since it was Fourth
   of July weekend and there were lots of families hiking, and he

said, "Oh, it isn't customary here?" He had some sort of accent
. . . definitely not French Canadian, but I couldn't tell what
it was.

(*Laughter, questioning.*)

Oh, yeah, no he had a backpack. And boots and socks. And he
started pulling out clothes right then.

(*Awe, laughter.*)

Retelling to Outsider

So Julia, my boss, is hiking along on the Fourth of July, pretty early
'cause that's, like, one of the busiest days of the whole year in the
Adirondacks and she wants to be sure to beat the crowd. She sees
this other hiker coming down the trail toward her, and she's a little
surprised 'cause it's so early and he's already been up the peak.
But as she gets closer, she notices . . . he's not wearing any clothes.
He's got a pack on, and he's got boots on, but no clothes. And it's
not like this is the middle of nowhere! There are like eighty hikers a
day on this trail! Anyway, so she goes right up to him and tells him,
"Look, it's the Fourth of July. There are going to be lots of people
hiking today, so you might want to put some clothes on." And he's
like, "Oh, it isn't customary here?" Like, somewhere in the world
it is customary to hike naked. I mean, he did have some sort of
accent, but seriously, have you ever heard of people hiking naked
anywhere? I dunno, but if it had been me, and I had seen a naked
man walkin' down the trail towards me, I would have gotten the
hell outta there.

Group Retelling

Seth (a veteran of the previous three summers): Yeah, and then
suddenly, she just took off her shirt . . . and I wasn't really sure if
she knew I was there, but I was just like . . . ummmm . . . maybe
I'll come back a little later.

Zack: Well, you know, Julia met a guy hiking naked once.

Seth: Yeah, I heard about that, yeah.

Zack: I just don't really understand what your logic is with that. It can't be comfortable. Like, what if you fall?

Me: Well, and he was wearing a pack, too. Imagine the pack rash you would get—

Libby: And then she just went right up to him—

Me: Only Julia could walk up to a random naked dude totally calm—

Libby: Seriously, I would have died laughing.

Me: I think I just would have hidden in the woods.

Zack: Anyway, she asked him to put clothes on, and he had some with him . . . he had some weird accent, right?

Libby: Yeah, and she said he thought it was totally normal to hike naked . . .

Seth: I've definitely never heard of people hiking naked anywhere before . . .

Strange temporality took a hold of the entire stewarding crew. Every two weeks we met, at the Loj or in Lake Placid, over breakfast or ice cream cones, and recounted our news. Libby told us she dreamed she had to stop terrorists who were trying to blow up Mount Marcy. Gina described the celebratory wine and cheese that a kind couple shared with her on top of Cascade. I'd have heard some of the accounts already on shared days off, and others would be new, and some we would retell from weeks past. Our stories got tangled like too many instruments in a small room, and although we tried to straighten them into some coherent melody, we went two weeks at a stretch without being a group and our timing got lost over time. At the next meeting, Libby forgot when her dream happened and told the story a second time, having added a few embellishments to the original theme.

We did see each other one-on-one at strange, irregular intervals. Nights when we got to share a tent with another steward were a welcome relief from loneliness and fear. We would talk late into the night, uninterrupted by the buzzing of cell phones. The silence held our conversations like gemstones; it made them clear, beautiful, precious.

I spent my days off with Libby and Gina. We roamed the local towns, driving too fast and breaking our speakers with bluegrass basses. Gina and I bought a half dozen cookies and a pint of milk for six dollars and were convinced it was the best deal ever. Libby and I had shower parties, playing music and singing terribly under the steaming streams of water that had never felt better than after five days of sweaty, muddy hiking. We lived or relived moments together, the first repetitions of the tales later told at meetings, and these shared stories were exactly what bound us so close.

Sam arrives on the fourth day of what will prove to be a week of non-stop rain. I've been pacing figure eights at the Phelps junction for so long that you can see my track in the mud. Here at treeline, there's some protection from wind and rain, but I was still so cold yesterday that I curled up on a rock and slept the day away, forgetting hunger and hypothermia. Sam's blue eyes recall sunny skies, and we play hand games for hours. On the hike out, she understands why I let out a desperate shriek when I fall ankle-deep into a puddle; she doesn't mention that my boots are already so wet that this last dunking really doesn't change anything.

Gina and I weed Seth's garden in the high heat at three. We bask in the drone of the bees and weave wildflowers into each other's hair. Later, we sit on the porch of a farm stall munching grapes and strawberries with relish that only the semi-starvation from months of daily hikes can garner. A car pulls into the lot, and its driver sidles up to us, clicking a picture with her camera under the pretext of chatting with us. She doesn't ask permission, just points, shoots, and walks away. We glance at each other skeptically, and only then realize that we, skin tanned in odd stripes from work, hair braided messily with wilting blossoms, have become, as they say, local color.

Zack stirs his pot of pasta while I start chowing down on my own dinner. I babble in frustration about a hiker who told me how surprised he was to find a woman steward up on Marcy. "I just mean that hiking's way easier for men," he told me, ignoring my presented evidence that five of the six summit stewards are women this summer. Zack listens to my rant and finally responds, "You know, I think at some point you just have to realize that people like that aren't gonna change, so I just ignore them 'cause they're idiots," taking me off guard as usual with his simple, perfect wisdom.

The Odyssey has a tendency to repeat itself, which feels heavy-handed to the high-schooler forced to read it cover to cover. It's a remnant of the epic's time as a purely vocal document, a history remembered through the spoken word. The repeated passages gave singers time to organize the upcoming sections, to pick points of emphasis and change tonalities to suit the audience at hand. For a crowd that loved blood and gore, they could draw out the battle scenes, or mostly skip them for gentler sensibilities. They could weave a different tale in each recital, while conveying the same message, the same great themes.

So when the stewards left the meeting table and returned to leaving notes and waving invisibly, we carried with us each other's stories. I carried Gina screaming in the dark tent at the Algonquin campsite, waking Libby with the terror of her nightmare. I carried Julia's partner kneeling on the Marcy summit in a suit, asking her to marry him as she threw her head back in laughter. I carried Sam sitting just above a short rock face on Cascade, laughing to herself as parents flustered and panicked, and their kids scampered up the face like it was made for climbing. Told and retold, these moments became an oral history. We formed bonds through storytelling that no longer exist in quite the same way in the world of texting and social media. The wilderness, empty of email and cell phones, gave us a chance to remember other ways of communication and communion.

At my college, where students give themselves scoliosis carrying their laptops around, even though their phones can serve as computer, GPS, and video-game system all at once, it can feel as though community depends on technology. Invitations to parties go out by e-mail. I find out about panels and workshops through Facebook. Texts inform me where to meet my partners for a group project. Remembering my time in the Adirondacks, however, also reminds me that love need not ride radio waves and friendship does not travel by fiber optics.

17

The Cage Canyon

* * *

JENNY KELLY WAGNER
2014, Winner

The first time I meet Kiya, she is chained to the passenger seat of a two-door Audi, glaring at me suspiciously with intense yellow eyes. When I approach the car, she cowers in the corner as far as the chain around her neck will allow. If I try to open the door, she might hurt herself struggling against the restraints in her attempt to get away from me, so I don't push my luck. I take a deep breath as the woman who chained Kiya to the seat steps out of the driver-side door.

Kiya is a two-year-old black wolf. I am a twenty-two-year-old blonde girl with a liberal arts degree who was never even allowed to own a dog as a kid, wearing filthy Carhartt jeans and a week's worth of grime. I live and volunteer at Mission: Wolf, a captive wolf sanctuary overlooking the jagged Sangre de Cristo Mountains in southern Colorado.

I have never seen a wolf in the wild. My ancestors, settlers from Europe, initiated the decline of the North American gray wolf by killing countless bison, elk, moose, and deer. Beginning in 1906, the U.S. Forest Service and U.S. Bureau of Biological Survey (now the U.S. Fish and Wildlife Service) sponsored a nationwide extermination of gray wolves to make grazing land safe for domestic cattle. Until 1965, a wolf carcass could earn you as much as fifty dollars from the U.S. government. At that time, a gallon of gasoline sold for thirty-five cents.

I wasn't alive in 1965, but my mother likes to say that our nation figured out a lot of things during the 1960s. As we were coming to terms with the diversity in our own population, the scientific community (and, perhaps more important, the National Park Service) was growing more confident that natural ecosystems became more healthy and stable as biodiversity increased. My mother, a stalwart feminist, joined the march on Washington, D.C., for civil rights in the summer of 1963. A year later, President Johnson signed the Wilderness Act. It would be ten more years before the Endangered Species Act forbade the hunting of our three hundred remaining wolves in northern Minnesota, and more than thirty years before the first wolves were reintroduced in Yellowstone National Park.

Before the government started releasing wolves into Yellowstone's Lamar Valley in 1995, overgrazing herbivores destroyed vegetation in our nation's first national park. Predators were scarce, and the grizzly bear was quickly disappearing from the unbalanced ecosystem. Once wolves returned, the oversized elk populations in the park had something to run from. Their hooves churned the ground loose, aerating the soil. After wolf reintroduction, plant life began to flourish. Young saplings in riverbeds could grow undisturbed by oversized herds of lazy ungulates. At least fifty species of songbirds returned to nest in the mature trees. Beavers built houses with willow branches. The shade from the trees cooled streams and rivers to a healthy temperature for fish, and the elusive grizzly bear started to make a miraculous comeback. Before the Europeans arrived, half a million wild wolves ranged across the continental United States. Now, a quarter of a million wolves live here in captivity, while fewer than ten thousand wild wolves roam our small patches of wilderness. Desperate for a connection to the wild, many people buy wild animals and take them home.

As I watch Kiya clawing at the Audi's upholstery, I am less concerned about what wilderness means for me than I am about what it means for her. People call us every week with horror stories of unruly pet wolves. Kiya's story is an all-too-familiar narrative. Sold as a puppy from a breeder in Canada who claimed she was 98 percent wolf, 2 percent dog, she was confined to a small apartment in a subdivision outside of Denver, terrified of everyone except the couple that raised her.

Kiya bit a young girl who tried to take a shoe away from her. Her next forty-five days must be spent in quarantine at our facility or she will be destroyed.

The first thing we have to do when we receive a phone call from a wolf or wolf-dog owner is take a deep breath. Usually, it's an emergency. *A wolf jumped my 8-foot fence and is running around on the interstate. A wolf attacked my wife's dog over the food bowl. My wolf thinks he is protecting me by growling at my partner. My neighbor saw how our wolf carries our two-year-old around gently by the head, and when he tried to intervene, the wolf got rough.*

Take the animal to the vet yourself and pay to have it euthanized, we tell people on the phone, because that is what will happen if you set it free or take it to a shelter. Be responsible. Make it quick and clean.

My job isn't always as grim as it sounds. In summer, I meet hundreds of kids from all over the country. My favorite groups are the inner-city kids who come up with a Denver nonprofit to camp next to our parking lot. They wear sweatshirts and baggy jeans instead of Gore-Tex shells. Most of them have never seen the stars. It takes them some time to get used to the silence, but after a week of sleeping outside, the kids learn to sit calmly and listen. I wonder if a week is enough. I wonder what the world would be like if adults all learned to sit calmly and listen.

Most of the meat we feed the wolves arrives in the form of donated livestock, animals at neighboring ranches that have reached the end of their lives. Our neighbors call us when they have a horse or cow go down (meaning that it either died in the night or has been recommended for euthanizing), and we bring it to the sanctuary to process, then feed to the wolves. Often, I find myself teaching anatomy lessons to curious visitors. I'm not a biologist. I yawned in the back of my high-school science class, daydreaming and skipping my homework until the glorious day we finally got to dissect a fetal pig. But a week ago, I found myself holding a large, bloody cow pancreas aloft, in front of a pack of fascinated thirteen-year-old Girl Scouts as they helped me prepare food for the wolves at our sanctuary. Humans are driven by a need for direct experience. Our souls crave what is raw and real, even if we have convinced ourselves we can opt out of all that nasty survival stuff. Instead, we watch, on the Discovery Channel, every other species worry about the circle of life.

We depend on wild plants and animals for our survival, and yet we do our best to cover up all evidence of our participation in the cycles of our natural world. My food has been deboned, pre-washed, and no longer resembles anything that thirteen-year-old girls think is cool. My drinking water comes from a pipe diverting Rocky Mountain snowmelt, via the Arkansas River, that used to flow all the way to Mexico. We are just as disconnected from soybeans as we are from cows, so do the moral implications change if I eat a steak or a piece of tofu? I want to hold the hatchet that beheads my chicken dinner. I want to hear the snap of spinach stems severed by my own pair of scissors. I want to reconnect.

I want to feel a connection to nature, but the twenty-foot-long chain connecting me to a black wolf named Kiya is not what I had in mind. I am holding a piece of the wild in my hands, and she wants nothing to do with me. As I begin to walk across the flat dirt parking lot, Kiya takes off running and almost pulls me off my feet. I direct her in circles, which she runs relentlessly around me. Kiya has no desire to come closer to me. I give her all the slack I can on the chain. At a fifteen-foot distance from me, she visibly relaxes. Finally, almost enough space.

The wilderness is shrinking. For wolves and other wildlife, how we manage the world's remaining wilderness could mean the difference between life in the wild and existence only in cages. I might never see the remaining pockets of untouched land, but their ecological value is inestimable. Much of our oxygen comes from places that we will never visit: huge swaths of forest in North America and Siberia, the biologically diverse Amazon rainforest, cold oceans rich with phytoplankton and seaweed. Our fates closely entwine with the rest of the earth, but humans live a disconnected existence. We surf the Internet instead of talking to each other. We pave the space between our feet and the ground so that we can drive past everything without having to feel the chilly air or listen to the birds or greet our neighbors. By insulating ourselves from the outdoors, we have created a cage for ourselves that is warm, comfortable, and lonely as hell.

By now I have known Kiya for three years, and she still doesn't want to hang out with me. All she wants from me is the whole leg of road-killed deer I'm carrying down the hill in a plastic bucket. Unable to build an appropriate fence, the woman driving the Audi had no choice but to ask us to take her wolf in permanently. She visited Kiya once, and the wolf spiraled into disappointment after she left.

Kiya now lives in a three-acre pen with two other canines. I feed her, and that's the reason she can never learn to survive in the wild. Because she was born in captivity (to a breeder in Canada), she thinks humans are the source of all her food.

At night, I fall asleep to the howling of Kiya and thirty-five other wolves, imprisoned for their own good inside fences up and down the canyon. Like Kiya, they do not know how to find their own food and cannot survive in the wild. I wonder if I'm very different. Outside the fences, a pack of wild coyotes yips in reply. The sound curbs my loneliness. Somewhere north of here, out of earshot from any human, a wild wolf is howling.

18

Walking with Our Faces
to the Sun

* * *

NANCY RICH

2014, Runner-up

 Jess and I pile on the down parkas and fleece for our wild-life tracking jobs. Typically it's zero degrees (or below) and our pace all day is, well, glacial, because we stop every few meters to record the tracks along two forest transects. This is not like the winter hiking that I know and love, where you get warm hauling body and pack up a peak. No, we're at the same 1,200-foot altitude all day in these Berkshire Hills of western Massachusetts, and we're stopping more than we're hiking. Each animal track we see requires GPS coordinates, photo, species identification, and pencil record on the data sheet. It's cold work, especially for the fingers. We do this for two full days after every snowfall.

Our project is part of a Nature Conservancy study of mammal activity in the wildlife corridor that stretches from Vermont down to the southern Appalachians. The two transects we prowl lie in an area of mixed private and state wildlife management land. One plot lies on a low wooded ridge, and the other sits beside a river. Our observations will help create a scientific foundation for future decisions on land conservation to preserve this wildlife corridor. Well into the winter, I am still in love with this job. I feel exceedingly lucky to get this close to the animals.

* * *

Depending on which definition of the Berkshires one uses, these hills rise 2,800 or 3,500 feet above sea level, lower than the White Mountains. I and approximately 800,000 other humans live in the Berkshires, and I haven't met a neighbor yet who doesn't value this beautiful land that is not quite wilderness—not a place where "man himself is a visitor who does not remain," as the Wilderness Act of 1964 specifies. But we routinely see black bear on our lawns, moose crossing winding roads, and the shine of foxes' eyes at night. The tracking project reveals that the animals live all around us, their tracks and sign and sometimes their bodies in plain sight when we fully open our eyes.

What is the word for this place? Is it wilderness? What other word is there? I propose to explore these questions by taking the reader on some tracking days as seen in excerpts from my journal.

November 29, 2013
The Ridge

Today we placed four motion-triggered wildlife cameras on our ridge transect at a very special place, a tiny sphagnum moss wetland in a trough between parallel walls of fractured schist. We observe dozens of piles of bear scat, most of it fresh and full of blackberry and raspberry seeds and beechnut shells. It seems late in the season for a bear to be moving around, but then we have had only a dusting of snow so far. Moose have paced this hideaway basin for weeks, maybe months, leaving their droppings, some old and sawdust-like, some fresh and shiny like malted milk balls. Gleefully, we expect to see the animals on the videos.

December 28, 2013
The Ridge

A beautiful blue-sky day, warm for December. Today, again, we are moving the cameras and still waiting for enough snow in which to track. Covering the same ground as before, I begin to realize the sheer variety of habitats. A cattail swamp below the ridge might house beaver. A rocky outcrop could provide dens for bobcat, while dense hemlock—huge trees overlooked by past logging crews and new growth—might provide the range of options for deer and moose.

Today's find: the most beautiful, elegant tracks of the season so far—fresh bear prints crossing black pond ice. The heat of the paws has melted off the thin covering of snowdust, making intensely visible every detail of toe and palm. The pattern is so humanlike—a sole with creases and lines in it, perfect for FBI fingerprinting, five oval toes. I think of stories about humans and bears being related, and I can see why: look at their footprints.

Every day I wonder whether I can complete this dream job. I'm older than most field technicians. I move slowly with aches and pains always lurking. Naturally I hope things will get better but, of course, I might just be a fool. But having finished the New Hampshire 4,000-footers in winter (and not that long ago either), I hope that one foot in front of the other will carry me through.

Saturday, January 4, 2014
The River

Finally a tracking day! Very cold—minus 7 to start, then warming. Cold advisories everywhere—radio, Internet, common sense. Five inches of light powder, plenty for tracking. Jess arrives to carpool in the pre-sunrise glow, grinning hugely as am I. "What a gorgeous day!" we call out. How else should one meet the challenge of such cold?

As we drive past the old potato fields on the way to our transects, a magnificent sunrise lights the sky in the west as well as the south. A glorious clear morning.

I must press eight times on the GPS touchscreen to take a photo and coordinates. Each pressing steals warmth from my fingertips. Jess, with the resilience of youth (or perhaps better gloves), fortunately says her hands are fine as she pencils in the mammal species, track direction, forest type and age, coordinates, photo number, waypoint, record number.

Not much is moving in the woods today. For the first time, we see no deer tracks at all. Maybe they hunker down when it's this cold, but where? Dense hemlock groves, probably, not the open beech woods.

Squirrels seem comfortable with the cold and the fresh powder, their tracks deep and big between trees. Mice skitter back and forth to dry plant stalks that still bear seedheads, leaving precise and dainty tracks—dots from their feet interlined with dashes from their tails. Coyotes have been cruising, three or four at a time along the riverbank, flattening the snow where they greet each other.

Later, we find the sharp-pointed tracks of red fox, identified to a certainty as Jess says, "Here, I'll scoop up the snow with the urine in it. You smell it. I have no sense of smell." "OK," I say agreeably, and am instantly sorry as the skunk-like stink reaches my nostrils.

We have our favorite spots now—the zone of bear and moose where we set up the four cameras, the ravine where porcupines cross to their rocky den, the spot of high animal activity by the road, where a hunter left a bloody track from hauling out a deer, and two fishers and a dog madly circled each other.

The woods, of course, are not a danger-free zone for the residents. Last time we found a squirrel carcass missing its head and feet. Raw bone stuck out from the leg fur. Today's grisly find is a mauled bird surrounded by coyote tracks.

The cold creates very special riverine sculptures. Bottom ice in the river shines greenish, with more ice shelving over it, and whirlpools and bubbling springs of water spreading above in waves and scallops. Frost feathers dot the river ice like clumps of bunchgrass, a pattern I have never seen before. We pause in awe.

River otters have been sliding down the banks, scooping channels on the snowy river ice. At the shore, they leave oozy, greenish-yellow secretions and their webbed prints. Their fish-scale-full droppings are absent.

I am eager to see the ridge transect tomorrow, especially where we found the elegant fresh bear tracks and the moose droppings.

Sunday, January 5, 2014
The Ridge

We are surprised and disappointed to find no fresh bear or moose sign today, and no moose on last month's videos. But the videos show a bear, wide awake and sniffing around the cameras. The moose have probably left for better eating, since their wetland plant food here is under ice, and the trees lack the fresh twig growth that moose like. Or perhaps they resented our failure to get their permission to photograph.

But the day offers new excitement: bobcat tracks! Clear as a handwritten signature, the tracks show the four oval toe pads and the three-lobed heel pad, a "ramp" sliding down into every print, and the "halo" around each track—an empty surround larger than the actual footprint, where the leg fur brushes out a funnel as the paw slides in. The trail reveals an animal who struts, right down the center of a ravine, down the center of a snowy woods road, swiftly changing intent and direction at will. A video underscores this impression, showing a bobcat stalking across an icy wetland on muscular legs.

Like the bobcat trails, coyote tracks also look purposeful, but these animals are long-distance hikers, heading in straight lines along the river, across iced ponds, along a ridge, or dipping down from the riverbank to snoop on the ice then gallop back up. Rarely have we found only a single line of coyote tracks; usually we see two, three, four, or more. Sometimes the tracks converge in a scuffle, perhaps in play or in greeting.

We like this ridge transect very much, especially the part that lies farthest from a plowed road and hints at the most secrets.

Deer and turkeys have trampled enormous areas—larger than

football fields—beneath hemlocks and beeches, seeking shelter and beechnuts.

We are seeing deer urine with blood in it, signifying a female in estrus. Apparently, few mammals give birth in January, but several species have their young in February and March. Likely they are working hard now to eat enough. I wonder what we will find—or notice—as the birthing season comes around.

I learn so much and feel so lucky to be doing this work. "Being there" in my job of intensive noticing makes me truly know this place. But because fieldwork also involves hard physical labor— not to mention heat, cold, poison ivy, sucking mud, briars, or bugs —I realize I may soon not be there. Calcium deposits and compressions of cartilage in my body are having their say. My falls after hooking a snowshoe on logging slash leave more damage now, despite the ever generous softness of the snow.

I will think about that later. In any case, the sleepless nights early in the project, when I despaired of handling the physical demands, have ended. Last night I dreamed of winter sunlight gleaming on young birch stems. When the trees enter my dreams, I know the border between myself and the woods is becoming permeable. I feel deep amazement and gratitude. I believe that just being there and paying attention is the way the barrier gets breached, and that's why I do this work. I am as surprised and incredulous as a teenager in love.

Today in the stillness, I heard murmuring from a porcupine den as we set up a camera nearby.

Friday, January 17, 2014
The Ridge

Jess is moving quickly toward a career as wildlife biologist. I am at the age when people retire, not when they start new careers. But I am enjoying being out here getting to know the land so deeply.

Today we pause to listen to the chickadees. Their calls come from constantly changing sites. These are birds who land, then flutter to another spot, then another and another. They voice their *chickadee-dee-dee* call, their *yoo-hoo*, their *tsk-tsk*-ing.

Each time we cross the ground, it looks different—a turkey scuffles in a new place, deer beds have become melted snowdust instead of deeply embossed ice. Today, more beechnut husks dot the snow.

We notice bobcat tracks in a new place, just outside the transect area, and a recent video shows a bobcat at yet another spot. I keep thinking about patterns—when and where the animals are moving, and how large an area they need for all the facets of their lives. The deer need dense hemlocks for cold-weather shelter, open beech woods for the nuts, and lichen-covered rocks for winter nibbling. For a few days, we find the bobcat evidence in a different place each time, and then we see it again at the first site. How many pairs are there? How much land do they need? So many things I don't know.

Tuesday, January 21, 2014
The Ridge

We have three companions today: our project director, a local reporter, and a filmmaker. It's very cold—the temperature fell below zero last night, and it's around zero this morning. Today's dress: six layers plus immense down parka. The reporter plies us with questions, and the filmmaker takes photographs. I say how much we are learning from the animals. Most of us who live here know which species are around because we see them sometimes, but probably few of us realize the great density of animals, let alone do we know much detail about their lives. They live as our neighbors but, for the most part, out of our sight.

Thursday, January 23, 2014
The River

We install two cameras by the water, hoping to photograph otters where we found their tracks last week. Camera placement is mainly by guess and intuition, and we are wrong as often as we are right. The animals must be going by feelings and rules I have no idea about.

Today abundant fisher, weasel, and mink tracks teach us the distinction between these cousins. The fisher is a straight-liner with a few gentle curves, while the weasel is a loop-the-looper with many passes in and out and around, investigating holes, logs, tree boles. The mink, intermediate in size, sniffs down by the river, winds back through the trees. We have learned from other animals, too: the bobcat that first time a few weeks ago, the bear crossing the pond ice with such elegance.

One morning my husband wished us well for the day, hoping we would "walk with our faces to the sun." I have come to see that my heart-healthiness depends on walking toward, and seeking to know, the animals and plants, the ridges and rivers.

Tuesday, January 28, 2014
The Ridge

We start in a temperature of eight below. My hands and feet are cold all day, and interior coldness will last all evening despite the woodstove. Today I will again ask myself whether I'm getting too old for this.

We see bobcat tracks again. What moves me most is the physicality of how each foot enters and leaves the snow, telling much beyond the shape of the paw—telling about the body, the coat, the energy.

Each day we shake hands with beech saplings (getting poked in the eye in return) as we pass through their territory.

Today the sunrise bursts over the potato fields again, and winking plays of green, yellow, purple, and orange light dot the snow.

Wednesday, January 29, 2014
The River

Another cold day, beginning around zero and ending at 18 degrees. We find lengthy runs of fisher tracks, and snowy river ice covered with the looping calligraphy of weasel tracks. The ice is spectacular —shelving, green, sparkling.

This river is federally designated as wild and scenic, meaning in essence that it's beautiful, though of course the enabling legislation speaks in other words. On one stretch, only twenty or so feet wide, ice cliffs on the banks rise an astonishing eight feet high, debris-filled and capped by waist-thick slabs that must have floated down in last week's 50-degree melt. The pile-ups give off the blue light I have seen in alpine glaciers. In the river itself, the ice light is green beneath the sheeting water. River sounds are muted until the water suddenly breaks free of the ice and drops over rocks. The layers and shapes of ice witness to the verbs of this winter: melting, swelling, freezing, opening, closing, bursting, subsiding. We speak quietly of our gratitude at getting to see this river week after week.

Why do the deer, otter, fisher, mink, and coyote travel on the ice? A few, often deer, are crossing to the other side, but most are not. They can't be finding much to eat out there and, except for the otter, the tracks do not generally lead to a drinking spot. But I suddenly realize I am underestimating the "humanity" of the animals (what is the word, in the case of a non-human animal?). Last night, for example, a full moon shone in an exceptionally clear sky; maybe the animals just like to see and play in the moonlight. It can't be true that their lives are limited to business, can it?

A breeze blows snow off branches, sending me the scent of old leaves quivering on the beech saplings.

Sunday, February 3, 2014
The River

The wildlife camera shows an otter sliding on the ice toward the river. Although otters are related to the loping fisher and the bounding weasel, they move in a completely different way, pulling themselves along by the front feet, as the back feet draw together by the tail, and their heavy, plump bodies heave and roll until they reach a gliding point. The fisher, though, darts—turning a quick and powerful body this way and that while inspecting the camera.

Along the riverbank we see fresh spots of blood every two meters or so, accompanied by coyote tracks. A video shows a coyote rolling in something on the snow, five times within the fifteen-second film, wriggling with the greatest glee I can imagine a coyote ever having. Perhaps it is his lady's estrus blood.

Suddenly the animals seem more individual. I am reminded that I too am animal, I too have had such blood spots, and the does and coyote mamas and I are deeply connected in that way. And now, unmistakably, I think of the coyote and the doe as "she," no longer "it." Robin Kimmerer talks in her book *Braiding Sweetgrass* about learning "the grammar of intimacy." Maybe I'm starting to do that.

Saturday, February 9, 2014
The Ridge

Finally enough snow for that silken downhill glide on our snowshoes! To our delight, we see that an otter too must have felt that joy of gliding, traveling right through the woods on a journey between wetlands a mile apart. We examine the trail closely, deciphering the direction, the marks where the paws provoke the body's slide through the trees, under a fallen log, up the other side of a dip. The otter must be vulnerable on an overland route, but perhaps the fighting and clawing instincts of fisher and weasel relatives run in the otter family as well.

I now have a *relationship* with this place. It has become "thou" instead of "it." That is why I do this work. I want to see the land where I live, hear it, feel it, smell it, be touched by the cold, follow my animal neighbors' doings. I want more than guidebook identifications; I want to hear the stories in the woods.

By paying attention, and being there, and considering animals as "he" and "she" and not "it," my hearing begins to come back. The structure of the project helps, carrying me through the dawn that catches me tired and sleepy, the day that feels tedious, the times when I doubt the value.

A friend tells me of her terror as her dog chased a black bear out of the yard and into a neighboring conservation area, the dog yelping and returning with claw-marked ribs. She is not impressed with my description of elegant bear tracks on the ice. Her story reminds me that the animals we track are not toys, pets, or aesthetic objects; it is well to remember that.

Tuesday, February 11, 2014

We do not track today. We're waiting for a big storm later this week, so I take this time instead to reflect.

I am coming to think of wilderness as a state of mind and relationship with intact ecosystems. I think of places with intact ecosystems as those areas large enough to have a buffer between human and animal territories. Large enough for animals to meet and greet each other, roll in their mate's estrus scent, cruise the woods in their particular gait for their own unaccountable purposes, live or die by the size of this year's beechnut crop. Large enough for giving birth and playing in the moonlight, for planting seeds through their droppings and nut caches. Far enough from humans' yards to avoid the snapping of territorial dogs.

I still need the larger wildernesses—the achingly beautiful ridge-lines of the White Mountains, the high passes and secluded tarns of the Sierras. But there is something here in the hills a half hour from my home that takes me out of myself and my everyday just as wilder lands have often done. This tracking project helps me see into a different world as I move quietly through the eating areas, the living spaces, the mating zones of these animals. This vision of another wilderness is about *being there* with my neighbors—the river and its ice, the chickadees, the otter and bobcat—and listening to them. And like the animals we have been tracking, I too need a range of habitats so I can choose what I need for a particular day, or season, or age.

19

Getting Lost in a Familiar Part of the Woods

* * *

AARON PICCIRILLO

2014

To look at a thing is very different from seeing a thing.
One does not see anything until one sees its beauty.
Then, and only then, does it come into existence.

OSCAR WILDE

 I was walking in early spring through familiar woods near my western Connecticut home. I had hiked this area of the woods so many times before that it felt as if I had every tree and rock committed to memory. Actually, I often drift into a kind of mental autopilot when hiking there. I have come to expect certain things of this place: I know the trees, the rocks, and exactly how long my usual loop will take. I can afford to get lost in my thoughts. Everything generally goes according to plan.

On that day, somewhere in the back of my mind, I am sure I was congratulating myself for getting out. I had been looking forward to connecting to my creative and inspirational source all week. My body and mind would be forged anew. The only problem was that, in reality, I could have been walking down a familiar sidewalk in New York City and my experience would probably have been the same. I went into autopilot mode. I became lost in the tumult of everyday thoughts: Have I been calling distant friends frequently enough? Did I offend anyone at that party last night? What were the details of that dream I had? I should write those down. Use them in a poem. Oh, and I needed to get something at the drug store on the way home . . . what was it again? On and on and on. After about half an hour, I found myself looking up into an unfamiliar area, not knowing quite where I was. It was a simple mistake. I had veered off the usual path.

Suddenly, I was not just on a routine hike in the woods. I was in a wild place. I felt a flash of exhilaration when I glanced up and realized the woods did not look how I expected them to look. I felt like a wild animal. The leaves shimmered more brightly, the scents of dirt and bark burrowed deeper into my lungs, and my wandering, unfocused thoughts instantly vanished. Instead, visions flickered in my mind: running through the woods as a child at dusk, prickers sticking to my pants. Looking at sunsets from a distant hilltop. Standing in damp, muddy fields, in March, hungry. Places I have never seen before shot like lightning bolts in my mind's eye. I don't know what they meant or why they appeared.

The feeling was of something mysterious and Other showing itself to me in a fleeting moment, in a part of the woods that would otherwise have been typical or commonplace if I had been hiking or exploring as usual. The forest became truly wild and alive, in all of its strangeness and its inability to ever truly be known.

After this moment passed, I brought my mind back into focus, looked to my right and my left, and chose a way back to the main trail. For the rest of my trek, my thoughts swarmed around that brief moment in which my thoughts had ceased and something had opened up around me. I recognized errors in how I had been relating to the forest. Initially, I felt that I understood those woods, that they were familiar and almost familial. The forest was not a mysterious other, it was a part of me, and I considered it my home away from home. It was always there for me in the same way, and I could always count on its permanence and predictability. It was a sanctuary, or a haven, and I walked through it ceremoniously. As Raymond Williams puts it, nature had become "a refuge, a refuge from man; a place of healing, a solace, a retreat."[1] I sought a spiritual antidote to the material life but, ironically, this led to a rigid routine that made a spontaneous relationship to the forest much harder.

When I found my way back to a familiar path, I looked down at the rocks I had seen hundreds of times before: rocks that perhaps, in the past, might have conjured thoughts of strength, permanence, and resolve. I looked at the trees, and I thought of what acorns had meant to me: the fragile beginnings of things, the majesty and strength that can come from nurturing and tempering oneself through a season of darkness. Perseverance. I looked at everything around me, and thought of all the meanings I had previously placed on the forest. All of those meanings had vanished in that brief moment when I had felt like a wild animal: when there was no meaning—only mystery and unknowing, and the rapid influx of the entire forest into all of my senses.

I came to realize that my preconceived notions of the forest, of what I would find in the forest, and even of what the forest is, had blocked my experience of the forest. It may seem odd to say that, but it is worth saying again: my idea of the forest blocked my experience of the forest, and it took getting lost to come to this realization. I had placed so much expectation and obligation onto nature to be what I envisioned it to be, that I may as well have been walking around in a mall, searching for a specific product that I knew would serve a specific purpose. When that expectation was short-circuited for a moment, I was not just looking at the forest, as Oscar Wilde might have said, I was seeing the forest.

Was I wrong to seek meaning in the forest, or was I merely projecting my desires and wishes onto the wild places around me? Is seeking meaning in nonhuman nature a valid way of relating to wild places, or does this place a responsibility on nature that it should not have to bear? As David Harvey has noted, saying "'nature knows best' is to presume that nature can 'know' something."[2] The tendency to project a static, human ideology onto the dynamic, non-human world is a common one. According to Raymond Williams, "the idea of nature contains, though often unnoticed, an extraordinary amount of human history."[3] How are we to experience nature, then, when it seems so easy to project our desires, fears, and ideological constructs onto it? What is left after the objectifications and expectations are removed? How can we properly relate to that which we cannot entirely know? I couldn't articulate these questions properly at the time, but I knew that something had changed.

* * *

A couple months later, I was back on the same trail. Crossing over a small brook, I came across the fresh shards of a large tree that had been struck by lightning. The inner bark was a light brown, free of any sort of blemish or discoloration. The pieces measured about four feet long, and they were very sharp. They did not look like they belonged in the middle of the forest. They looked too perfect, almost as if they had been crafted by an artist and belonged in a museum. My first thought was to gather up five shards and plunge them into the ground, in a semi-circle, for no particular reason. One piece was bigger than the others, with a semicircular mass of wood extending from the top, a section that must have been wrapped around the base of a branch. I placed this shard in the middle of the other four. It looked like a giant eye. Happy with my makeshift installation, I stepped back, put a few finishing touches on it, and continued on my way. I looked back to see how it looked from a farther distance. It looked good. I imagined other people walking by, lost in their everyday thoughts, looking straight ahead and missing it. Then, I imagined hikers who might randomly look to the side of the trail just at the right moment, only to find the sculpture staring back at them. I had not assigned any meaning to creating the sculpture, but I walked away feeling that I had just cultivated a new relationship with the woods.

Reframing my experience of the forest as one of relationship, rather than seeing the forest as a tool or an object to be used for a purpose, made a difference for me. Now I am less frustrated if I don't happen to have a profound experience every time I hike. When I walk these paths now, I observe what is around me, but I do not actively attempt to extract meaning, as if the forest were a novel. I do not expect to gain anything specific, nor do I get disappointed if a bad mood lingers and everyday thoughts do not cease. The path will still be there next time and, on better days, I may dissolve into the essence of things, or become unexpectedly inspired, for an unknown reason. I will be that wild animal again. But I make no demands and expect nothing. In the meantime, I focus on the trees, and the rivers, and the rocks, and I acknowledge their otherness. I admire their beauty, and perhaps even take a picture or two, but I do not attempt to own their essence. I do not know what they mean. Every so often, something opens up and that strange feeling breaks through, or I get a peculiar urge to do something like create a sculpture from shards of wood. I do not know why, or how. Weeks may pass until this happens again, but I do not expect it, or become upset with the forest when it does not happen.

* * *

The wild places near my home have felt familiar and yet also strange for a long time. And now they are stranger still. They no longer fit neatly into the same categories I once placed them in, and they do not exist solely for my personal well-being, aesthetic tastes, or spiritual aspirations. They have become more than just the recharge center of my life. Now, I relate to them—not on my terms, or on their terms, but somewhere in the middle. The trails I once walked so rigidly and ceremoniously I now walk more playfully. I find more space and more room to breathe. I allow for something unexpected to wander in. Sometimes, when I wander off the path, or when the tumult of thoughts cease and the wild animal takes over, a type of communication takes place with the forest, and the relationship I have with the wilderness evolves. The path wanders on to me, and the phenomena that have no names, categories, or trails running through them burrow themselves into my thoughts and actions. And they remind me of something important I have forgotten.

NOTES

1 Raymond Williams, *Problems in Materialism and Culture* (London: Verso, 1980), 80.
2 David Harvey, *Justice, Nature, and the Geography of Distance* (Oxford: Blackwell Publishers, 1996).
3 Williams, *Problems in Materialism and Culture*, 67. See also Raymond Williams, *Keywords: A Vocabulary of Culture and Society* (New York: Oxford University Press, 1983), 219–24.

20

One Tough Gal

* * *

DOVE HENRY

2015, Winner

My palms and forearms felt fragile, scraping against the jagged rock I carried to my half-built cairn. I added the stone to my growing pile of material and looked at the structure for a moment, contemplating where to place the new piece. People like to talk about feeling insignificant in the face of a starry sky, but I think looking down at the earth offers a much closer dose of perspective. There is nothing like a billion-year-old rock to remind you of your own brevity. The Adirondacks are full of them. As a geological event, the formation of the range was actually more recent than what formed other Northeastern ranges, which belong to the older, eroding Appalachians. The Adirondacks are still moving up. They stand at the southernmost part of a shield that forms the ancient core of the North American continent: all Precambrian rock stretching up through Quebec into Greenland. New Yorkers refer to the region as the North Country, which I always liked because it reminded me of the Bob Dylan song about the girl with the warm coat and the long hair, *where the winds hit heavy on the borderline.*

Behind my cairn and beyond the summit of Algonquin Peak, layers of altitude colored the landscape. The gray summit of Wright Peak emerged boldly from a band of spiky, dark pines, which bled into the mixed deciduous forest below. Birch leaves glittered shades of green and gold in the wind. One of my favorite parts of hiking an Adirondack peak is experiencing the terrain change—noticing the birches and maples trailing off into conifers, stumbling across larger and larger patches of gleaming bedrock, feeling the wind pick up and the temperature drop in a crescendo toward the summit. I love that exhilarating moment when you begin to escape from the treeline and catch the first glimpses of the world below you.

The day was so clear I could even see the lighter green of faraway fields and the black of asphalt roads, cutting distinctly human lines and angles in the distance. A middle-aged man and his two daughters hiked past me a few yards away.

"You go, girl!" he shouted at me, smiling.

I politely smiled back. This was my second summer working on a trail crew in the Adirondacks, and I had heard that phrase before. I liked it better than, "Do you need some help with that?," which I had also heard on occasion. But even this man's well-intentioned words bespoke a subtle and deeply ingrained condescension that has become familiar to me as a woman working in wilderness areas.

I looked away from the summit, toward my three male coworkers building their own cairns below me. They were the only humans I could see, but they seemed to belong to the terrain, as if they were composed of the same stuff. Each man wore pants softened and stained by earth, and each was shirtless, baring torsos browned by the sun and hardened by labor. I watched one place a rock on his almost-finished cairn, which stood at least to the shoulder of his six-foot-four-inch body. I bet no one ever asked him if he needed help. *well? lets be realistic*

Humans measured and built the roads, fields, and towns I could see from the summit of Algonquin Peak, imposing hard lines of human order on an otherwise chaotic landscape, making it usable. James C. Scott describes these techniques of reduction from a historical and political perspective. "In order for officials to be able to comprehend aspects of the ensemble, that complex reality must be reduced to schematic categories," he writes. "The only way to accomplish this is to reduce an infinite array of detail to a set of categories that will facilitate summary descriptions, comparisons, and aggregation."[1] Scott calls this "legibility." Humans have constructed similar schematic categories to make sense of their own bodies and minds—to make the wild human landscape legible.

But the natural world has often proved too dynamic and powerful for our efforts to control, know, and order it. It heaves up through the asphalt of roads, makes its soil dry and unusable after too many seasons of the same crop. It eats away at the ideas and expectations we have for particular categories of people—categories, like gender, that we have created to know and control each other. So many of these ordering systems that we hold in our heads are stripped away by life in the wilderness, where the disorder and infinity that underlies everything is left in its raw physical form. The wildness exists also in human-built areas, just beneath the veil of order. You can see it creeping up through the cracks in the sidewalk.

People often react peculiarly to the sight of a woman working in wilderness areas. It often surprises them, or confuses them. It worries others—the idea of a woman out in the backcountry, all by herself. In my four seasons working for the Adirondack Mountain Club, as few as three and never more than five women have worked on the sixteen-person trail crew. Trail-building requires directly and deliberately altering land that we otherwise try to protect from the human hand, and this makes it a unique form of stewardship. Of course, the trails themselves, and the structures along them, were carefully designed and created to minimize human impact on wilderness areas. Stone staircases anchor soil in steep areas that would otherwise become gullies. And water bars prevent erosion by diverting water off the trail. The job demands a tremendous amount of physical strength and stamina. On this front, men generally have an upper hand, given their taller, larger frames. However, physical strength means little if one does not understand how and when to use it. Like all forms of stewardship, trail-building also requires intelligence and humility.

Humility is essential to wilderness stewardship, and it is an uncommon virtue in the civilized world. Understandably so—towns and cities are crowded with our own recent fingerprints and footsteps. It's easy to forget that, at one time, we were not here—that things were not the way they are now. It's easy to look around and think, Yes. We built this. I am part of this. It is here because of me and it is here for me. But once, here, protozoa lived and squirmed and photosynthesized in hot, algae-filled seas in the most inhuman ways. The moon loomed so close to the earth that it pulled the tides 1,000 feet high. And magma squeezed through sediment deep in the alien regions at the center of the earth. Working on top of Algonquin, I was reminded of it every day by the thick, raised ribbons of igneous rock that glistened darkly on the summit. The veins were even harder than the anorthosite they cut across, even more impervious to the weather. They humbled me as I felt the ancient rock beneath my hands. Worn down by eras of creeping sheets of ice, the rain, the wind, and now my own fingertips. By comparison, my fingertips seemed infinitesimal, my whole body a soft, warm, fleeting organization of matter.

The sunlight ebbed, and I watched my shadow lengthen across the bedrock of the summit. My cairn grew, though not as quickly as I had hoped. The physical lack of human order becomes very apparent when working with native materials to build a structure such as a bridge, stone staircase, water bar, or cairn. Each piece of lumber or stone has its own set of irregularities, requiring extensive adjustments and readjustments to sit stably on what is probably an equally irregular surface. There is nothing that can be measured, and little that can be cut to fit perfectly—no squares or rectangles or other easily nameable shapes. It's more interesting that way, I've found. Working with dimensional lumber always requires some form of dense monotony—measuring and sawing decking, chiseling identical notches all morning and afternoon.

I ran my hand across the surface of my current problem stone, feeling the sections where it swelled and sharp spots where it had cleaved, taking note of each nub, lump, and depression. It takes a special type of knowledge to work with native materials. And it takes an extraordinary amount of patience.

"FOOOOOO!"

I heard my coworker and crew leader howl from the base of the summit, signaling the end of our workday. The sound evaporated quickly in the great expanse of air. The sun was now low in the sky, and I felt a sudden chill as a gust of wind cooled the sweat on the back of my neck. I pulled my hair out of its ponytail to keep my ears and neck warm. My nostrils filled with the smell of campfire smoke. Woods perfume. Hurriedly pulling my fleece over my head, I abandoned the harsh rocks and wind of the summit for the comforting trees below.

During our five days building cairns, our crew of four camped at MacIntyre Falls nearly two miles down slick rockslides, roots, and steep cobble from the work site. That week on Algonquin remains in my memory with the stark clarity that comes from being on an exposed summit. Each day felt like an inhale and exhale, moving up and out of the woods with the sun, watching it carve across the sky as the day swelled with the morning. And then it would recede, and we would descend into the forest again, accelerating the darkening day. The hike each morning and evening was long enough to get lost in thought, and I became completely entrenched in my own brain on the way up and down. There are wild and distant places inside us all.

On the way back to camp, I meditated on the remarks I had heard that week. My coworkers and I encountered more hikers in one day working on Algonquin than we did in a whole week at most of our projects. My female presence seemed to run contrary to many people's expectations of wilderness trail workers, as well as their expectations of the women they might encounter in the wider world. "You're one tough gal!" an older man had told me that afternoon, resting his elbow on his knee to catch his breath on his way up the steep summit. *Yes, I am pretty damn tough*, I thought to myself. *A lot tougher than you and most of the men I've seen this week.* A feeling of childish indignation swelled in my chest as I remembered the moment. It felt kind of like the day I learned that I couldn't play baseball anymore because girls played softball in junior high. Why did my presence on the summit make me a tough gal and not just plain tough? Why is a woman working in the wilderness more rare and impressive than a man doing the same thing? be real - your

bitter

If one looks back on the history of the idea of wilderness, it is not particularly surprising that men dominate careers in public land management and wilderness stewardship. The history of American wilderness is, like many histories, full of men. In the American environmental imagination, it was born as a place explored and managed by rugged frontiersmen with "fine, manly qualities," in Teddy Roosevelt's own words. These wilderness men lived a "hard and dangerous" existence outside of civilization, he wrote. Wild lands required men who were "brave, hospitable, hardy, and adventurous."[2] Well into the twenty-first century, the concept of wilderness has proven difficult to extract from what many still regard as traditionally masculine qualities—gritty toughness and physicality, fearless independence and strength.

Just as wilderness is a place historically regarded as masculine, so too have the ideals of femininity been deemed something far from wild. As long as mainstream expectations of the ideal female body persist—that it should be well-groomed, clean, soft, hairless, and delicate—wilderness areas will appear hostile to the physical work of female bodies. Although the last half-century has witnessed American women moving out of the home and into the workplace, we probably picture the financially independent career woman more often with lipstick and heels than with biceps and boots. Her independence and power are not derived from the strength and power of her body. The movement of women into the workplace has largely occurred within the confines of cushy civilized places, where structures exist to ensure the populace can meet its physical needs with some level of ease and comfort. Instincts are displaced. People live at a distance from their bodies as wild entities.

But living and working in the wilderness catapults even twenty-first-century human beings back into their animality. Just before we reached camp, my friends and I paused to rinse our hands and faces in the pools of icy water below the falls. I sat and straightened my legs, reaching toward my muddy toes to feel my back stretch and my hamstrings tighten. I could feel the change in my calf muscles after a few days up and down Algonquin, and my leg hairs had become bleached and softened by the sun. My stomach felt hollow with hunger after the hike down, and I suddenly realized I was ravenous. The most prominent sensations during a trail crew workweek are not specific to gender—hunger, exhaustion, heat, cold, disappointment, or satisfaction at the work and weather. After a few weeks in the woods, far from the memory and history that saturates human-built places, I think I identify more as a human or even as a mammal than I do as a woman specifically. It becomes very apparent how the reductive categories of gender—the qualities we ascribe to men and women and the summary descriptions we provide for each—are just as human-built as the roads that traverse a dynamic natural landscape.

The most obvious duality out there is that between what is human and what is not. And after some time living and working in the backcountry, it becomes clear that even the line between the human and the wild is also an invention. In remote outdoor areas, we become more astutely aware of the wilderness that remains within our own bodies and minds, regardless of the gender we experience culturally. It is not that this wilderness within us is absent when we live and work in places other than protected lands—far from it. But the human-built world so often serves to stifle or shun the wild. It is difficult to revel in the beauty of what is unknowable within ourselves when it is so profitable for others to claim to us that it is known. To face our own wildness, and to embrace it, is to be a true steward of wilderness.

NOTES

1   James C. Scott, *Seeing Like a State: How Certain Schemes to Improve the Human Condition Have Failed* (New Haven: Yale University Press, 1998).

2   William Cronon quotes these passages from Theodore Roosevelt's *Ranch Life and the Hunting Trail* (Century, 1889), in "The Trouble with Wilderness, or, Getting Back to the Wrong Nature," a chapter in his book, *Uncommon Ground: Toward Reinventing Nature* (New York: Norton, 1998), 100.

21

Lady and the Camp

* * *

ERICA BERRY

2015, Runner-up

 Anna's braces fell off after breakfast on the fifth day. I was rolling my rain jacket into my backpack when she came up to me, clutching them in her rosy palm—tiny metal pieces that had once been on her tiny ivory teeth. "Cricket," she said, "They've been loose for a while. I think we need to go to an orthodontist." Part of the chain was still in her mouth, and she cocked her head at me, smiling through wire and chapped lips, her cheeks a sunburned topography of mosquito bites.

I was leading a backpacking trip for middle-school girls through the alpine streams, granite outcroppings, and Indian paintbrush meadows of the Centennial Mountains of Montana.

At around four o'clock that morning, my co-guide had left on horseback to evacuate the ever-vomiting Mary. When I awoke, sweat-drenched, a few hours later, I was clutching my bear spray like a talisman in the mesh cave of my tent.

Now, a pair of alien hands rummaged through my pack: dirty fingernails, swollen knuckles, bug-bitten palms, branch-scratched wrists, a rainbow of friendship bracelets. I put Anna's braces in a Ziploc bag, telling her we would call for advice when we got back to the van.

I told her I had once accidentally thrown my retainer away with a paper plate, and finding it had required a dive through a dumpster full of pizza crusts and used napkins. She laughed behind wet eyes.

Propping my hulking backpack against a tree, I wiggled into the straps. I had just finished my freshman year at college in Maine, where I considered myself a comfortable outdoorswoman. I had learned how to dig a shelf for a tent in a steep snowbank. I trusted the rope when rappelling backward off cliffs. I swam through rock-choked rapids when pitched out of a canoe. I felt my torso scrape gravel as a flipped kayak dragged me downstream. Now, being responsible for the girls had let me re-learn my fears. Nausea swelled when I ran through the mental checklists of daily to-dos and to-avoids. When I thought of grizzlies and lightning and rattlesnakes and rock-fall and bee stings causing anaphylactic shock, I thought immediately of the girls: their gap-toothed smiles, their miniature hiking boots, their laughter at learning to poop in the woods. I also thought of their parents, sitting on sunporches around the country, gripping their smartphones and waiting for camp blog updates.

Ahead of me, twelve faces peered through pine needles and sunlight. The girls were grinning, kicking their feet like ponies in the trail. Behind them, above the horizon, a knot of black clouds shadowed a row of snowy summits. I wondered if I was living up to my camp name: Cricket, stolen in a crunch of indecision from our family's miniature Australian shepherd. After two sessions, I could almost forgive myself for answering to it. We had named her the first day we got her, after watching her hop through a meadow of thick grass that towered above her head. Her inability to know where she was going did not stop her from vaulting forward. She was an ankle-nudger, a gentle herder. She perpetually wagged the tail that she did not have.

"All ready, crew?" said a strange, strong voice beneath my ribs.

"Come on, Cricket," said Astrid. "We're following you!"

*　*　*

A few weeks after Christmas 1985, my mother's younger brother shot himself in the head. He was not yet my uncle—twenty years old, while my mother, at twenty-two, was just younger than I am now. He exists only as a photograph for me: a silent, floppy-haired Brady Bunch boy, flannel-shirted, outdoorsy. A year before his death, Ladd had cut many of the ties to his parents and flown to Alaska, where winter meant a weak, bleak five hours of light a day. Some weeks after his death, my mother received a package from his friends in the mail. Among the odds and ends were two postcards with her name on them. They were not dated, and his handwriting fell across the body of the cards leaving no room for an address. "I'm doing very well," he wrote. It seems clear that he did not intend to send them. His friends arranged his funeral, and neither my grandparents nor my mother ever saw that town of Dillingham, Alaska, where Ladd had spent the last eighteen months of his life.

Growing up, Alaska was almost a non-word in my house. When Sarah Palin came along, I secretly thanked her for giving us a new way to talk about the state. It was easier to say the name with a caricatured drawl. It was easier to marvel at the escapades of her Wasilla family than to think about our own links to that frozen appendage of the continent. The outdoor camp for girls that I worked for ran one session each summer in Alaska, and the description used words like "rugged," "truly competent," "rip-roarin'," and "adventuress." When I learned I had been assigned the Montana sessions instead, I couldn't decide if I felt relief or disappointment.

In high school, on a backpacking trip with friends, I read Jon Krakauer's Into the Wild, the narrative of college graduate Chris Mc-Candless, who donated his life savings to charity, hitchhiked the country, and was found dead in a rusted blue school bus in Denali National Park. The weed-snarled vehicle has become a sort of shrine in Alaska, and at least one person has drowned in the roar of a snowmelt river trying to tag it. Among my guy friends, the book circulated like a dog-eared bible, tucked in backpacks next to Jack Kerouac and John Steinbeck. It is impossible to separate the story of McCandless's adventures from the story of his death, but the line between reverence and repulsion is blurry. He followed his dreams. He found salvation in the wilderness, and then it killed him.

The McCandless fantasy is especially easy for young men. Perhaps this is because, unfortunately, solo travel is harder for women. It is tempting to fantasize about burning your credit card, hitchhiking through the desert, reading Edward Abbey, letting facial hair sprawl across your boy-man face. The difference, of course, is that, unlike McCandless, you could do it right. Call your parents from truck-stop pay phones every few weeks, weather the winter with large supplies of lentils and oats, know how to carve and cure the animals that come across your path. You would not die. You would become a legend, not a parable.

Returning from the backpacking trip, I struggled to tell my mother that I, too, had found myself absorbed in McCandless's story. "I just have no desire to read it," she told me. "It's too sad." McCandless died a different death than Ladd. He was sick, starving, and solo, though the controversy over his cause of death lives on. His story was part Jack London and part Greek tragedy—McCandless's hubris, his unfounded confidence in his primitive survival skills, betrayed him. And yet, there are some similarities between him and my uncle. They were born within four years of each other, and they both died, alone, in the cold darkness of an Alaskan winter twenty-some years later. Both left their families, and neither wrote nor called. "Some people feel like they don't deserve love. They walk away quietly into empty spaces, trying to close the gaps of the past," McCandless wrote in his journal. In photos I have seen of Ladd and McCandless, they are each wearing green-and-black check flannel shirts.

There is something masculine about going off the map, a desire for Thoreauvian self-reliance best discovered beneath the pines, within the proud drum of your own heartbeat. After McCandless's death, Chris Medred wrote in the *Anchorage Daily News* that "the

Alaska wilderness is a good place to test yourself. The Alaska wilderness is a bad place to find yourself."

Our society loves narratives of wilderness redemption. The stories go like this: run away from something that scares you, and you will run into something better. There is a brutal, literal logic in this. When I applied for the summer wilderness guide job, I did it because I, too, wanted to escape from zippers of red-light traffic and the blur of mindless social interactions. I wanted to breathe sage and cedar, see the West, and trust the sinews of my legs. But if I went into the wild to uncover something just as primal as McCandless, it was not about being alone. I did not want to disappear, and I did not think I would find myself. I just wanted people to rely on me, and I wanted to show them they were right to do so. I wanted to practice being a mother.

* * *

On family backpacking trips, my father used to crawl from the tent to boil water for us in the pre-dawn birdsong. When the water was hot, he would unzip the tent flap and hand my mother, sister, and me coffee or hot cocoa in blue-and-white speckled tin cups, singing his good mornings. He is not a man who talks very much about what spins through his head—he is slow to share both frustration and praise—and this particular action stands out to me as particularly character defining. It reveals a tenderness that, while far from dormant in the city, swelled in the mountains.

Later, when my sister's and my feet would slow under the weight of our packs, he would slither a lemon drop out of its plastic wrapper, coaxing us on. This was not a gendered caring—it was not because we were girls—but it was a parent's caring. I don't know if I knew it at the time, but it made me want to be a better person. It did not take long for my appreciation of the wilderness to blur with my appreciation for those glimmering versions of ourselves it offered back to us.

We refer to "human progress" as that trajectory of inventions to make life easier. We want to eat, drink, travel, and sleep better. We also want to love and communicate and die better.

Capitalism assures us that these two aims are tied: buy this new potato-peeler, and you will become a better mother. The mountains do not promise this. They ask a lot: competence, reverence, humbleness, and curiosity. In return, they blister and bruise and burn us, and somewhere—in that economy of dry oatmeal and the Milky Way, thunder and a hawk's solemn flight—they thrill us.

We talk about "re-wilding" our landscape: digging up fields, planting trees, bringing back wolves and owls. We also talk about re-wilding our diet: Paleolithic posturing, forgoing tortillas and oranges. But re-wilding our lives: what does that look like? I am wary to romanticize the pre-historic, pre-industrial, pre-Apple eras, because life is better now, for many more than me.

But each time you embark on a new adventure outside, you are given a chance to recalibrate yourself. There is something quietly invigorating about finding your bodily limits—wet feet, gnaw of hunger, a no-see-um bite. You pinpoint discomfort, and then you decide whether or not you will ignore it. Outdoors, you do this over and over again.

*   *   *

In high school, armed with an ice ax in an outdoor group full of adolescent boys, I learned to ignore more than just physical pain. I recalibrated myself socially, trying to compartmentalize gender. I was pale and scrawny, with fears of heights and snakes and hypothermia, so I picked my battles. As the male majority jostled to out-hike and out-joke one another, I joined in. I had never had brothers, and I liked this new sort of companionship. If I was lonely, I convinced myself I was not. I perfected a five-second pee behind bushes and rocks and in wetsuits. Once, after contributing to a post-curry burping contest, a friend remarked that I had "really let myself go."

He said it with mock horror and an appraising grin. What he meant, of course, was that after our time in the mountains, I had let the "feminine" go. My hair was twisted into week-old braids, and my face was wind-chapped and makeup-free. I remember feeling unsure about whether I should feel proud or insulted. In letting myself go—in leaving the performance of conventional girlhood back in the city—I wondered if I had lost something.

The camp I guided for in Montana embraced girlhood at 5,000 feet above sea level. Each night before bed, we gathered in a circle with a rainbow of nail polishes, awarding various "nails" to different girls: accolades for extra help, extra toughness, extra good jokes. We had impromptu dance parties on dirt roads, stopping the car and putting on tutus and crowns to dance to Taylor Swift on a barbed-wire stage. We howled at the top of summits and we sat in daisy meadows fielding the girls' questions about boyfriends in the "real world." I was surprised how little I missed the low-voiced chuckles of my male hiker friends from college and high school.

Before this, I had camped with an all-female group only once— when I was eleven years old, at a weeklong "empowerment" camp on a plot of forest and meadow in western Oregon. One morning, we stared at a tampon dissolving in a bucket, and then we bird-watched while the counselors shared livid descriptions of ob-gyn examinations. The director—a woman who walked in a halo of patchouli and wild gray hair—warned us to carry pepper spray whenever we were with men and sent us into the forest to glean wisdom from nature's goddess. I remember crouching against thick bursts of ferns, nested beneath a blue sky cut from the pine branches, waiting for my spirit animal while I tried not to cry. Needless to say, I did not leave with a deeper love for the trees, the eagles, or myself.

During one of my last days guiding in Montana, Jill, who was just a few years younger, broke down. She had attended the camp once before, and had been slotted to become an intern the following summer, but she was ready to go home. She missed her boyfriend. The hiking hurt. The guides were not allowed to be one-on-one with a camper unless we were in sight of the rest of the group—a lawsuit-preventative measure that I always heeded with another paranoid twist of fear—and I remember the two of us, sitting in soft pine needles by the side of a stream, watching as the other girls screeched and bucket-washed their hair in winter snow-melt. We joked, and we compared bug bites, and then we talked about our hike the day before: big summit, big views. She admitted she had been pleased with herself.

"But I could never do what you're doing," she said. I had laughed. I could only make sense of my summer in superlatives: it was the most rewarding thing to watch teenage girls learn to love the mountains, and learn to love themselves. But I was a teenager too then. It was the hardest thing to worry about whether I trusted myself shepherding them. I told some watered-down version of this to Jill, and she laughed at me.

"Oh Cricket, that's not even what I mean," she said. "Really, it's just your feet! They're disgusting. A whole summer! I could never do it." I followed her eyes down my bug-bitten legs all the way to my feet: zig-zagged with Chaco tans, the heels raw with shrunken blisters, toes wrinkled from sweat-soaked hiking socks, nails broken and purpling from boot pressure, echoes of chipped nail polish. They hadn't even registered with me. Suddenly we were laughing, both of us, doubled over in the late-afternoon sun, until our eyes pooled and our bellies ached.

That night, I would sit cross-legged with the girls and coat my toenails in a garish shade of glitter polish. The next morning, I would pull on wool socks, easing my feet into leather boots. We would put our lives on our backs and hit the trail, telling jokes extra loudly to warn the bears. Afternoon clouds would form, and they would thicken or disperse. And if the path got steep, and I heard the first whines of doubt, I would reach into my pocket, searching for the hard, slippery plastic of a lemon drop.

About the Contributors

KIMBERLEY S. K. BEAL ("Climate Change at the Top") now lives with her husband, children, and in-laws on Daisychain Farm in Belfast, Maine, where they grow and sell certified organic fruit and care for a hundred hens. Most of her energy goes into designing and running the farm, but she can quickly escape up to Katahdin or Acadia for a granite summit fix.

ANNIE BELLEROSE ("Introduction") is a writer and Vermont native who managed the Waterman Essay Contest for its first several years. She has explored and worked in the Northeast's mountains, earned an MFA in creative writing from the University of North Carolina-Wilmington, and now teaches writing at Champlain Valley Union High School in Vermont. Her work most recently appeared in *Rooted: An Anthology of Arboreal Nonfiction*, published by Outpost19.

ERICA BERRY ("Lady and the Camp") was raised in Portland, Oregon, and graduated from Maine's Bowdoin College, where she fell in love with the sea and mountains of New England. Her writing can be found online at *The Rumpus*, *The Columbia Journalism Review*, *The Atlantic*, *The Morning News*, *High Country News*, and *Guernica*, among others. She's currently a fellow and MFA candidate in creative nonfiction at the University of Minnesota in Minneapolis. You can reach her at www.ericaberry.com or @ericajberry.

BLAIR BRAVERMAN ("On Being Lost") lives with her fiancé and eighteen huskies on a farm in northern Wisconsin, where she is training for the Iditarod. Her first book, *Welcome to the Goddamn Ice Cube: Chasing Fear and Finding Home in the Great White North*, is out now from Ecco/HarperCollins.

KATHERINE DYKSTRA ("A Place for Everything") has published essays in the *Washington Post*, *Crab Orchard Review*, *Shenandoah*, *Gulf Coast*, and *Poets and Writers*, among other publications. Her essay, "Like Held Breath," was one of three finalists for the 2014 John Guyon Literary Nonfiction Prize. The same piece was included in the notables section of the 2015 *Best American Essays*, edited by Ariel Levy. The nonfiction book she is working on was flagged by Creative Capital, which called her an "artist to watch." She is contributing editor at *Guernica*. She lives in Brooklyn with her husband, Parker Chehak (who makes an appearance in her essay), and their two children.

DIANNE FALLON ("Hunting the Woolly Adelgid") is a writer and English professor at York County Community College. She grew up in suburban Boston, graduated from Bowdoin College, served in the Peace Corps in Morocco, and earned a doctorate in creative writing from Binghamton University. She is author of *Pioneer on a Mountain Bike* (Piscataqua Press, 2014). She lives in Kittery Point, Maine.

DOVE HENRY ("One Tough Gal") grew up in the fields and forests of the northern Catskills. She spent five summers working for the Adirondack Mountain Club, first as a naturalist, and then building trails with the club's professional trail crew. In May 2014, Dove graduated from Reed College with a degree in Environmental Studies–History. Since then, she has worked as a history teacher, dorm parent, waitress, trail crew leader, wildlife surveyor, maintenance technician, and ranch hand. She currently lives in the Bitterroot Valley of western Montana, where she continues to write about the natural and human environment.

WILL KEMEZA ("Dark Night on Whitewall") worked for several years in the White and Green Mountains and also thru-hiked the Appalachian Trail. He studied English at Boston College, earned a master of divinity degree at Harvard Divinity School, and now is an English teacher at Concord High School in Concord, Massachusetts, where he grew up and where he lives with his wife and children.

Shortly after writing "A Ritual Descent," JEREMY LOEB relocated from the craggy White Mountains to the Sierra Nevada. He worked in marketing and graphic design for a while, and now is pursuing a graduate degree in biological engineering, which he says will allow more time for playing in the mountains.

SALLY MANIKIAN ("It's a Seasonal Life") has now written several essays for *Appalachia*, for whom she also serves as "News and Notes" editor. In the past decade she's worked as reporter, adjunct professor, community organizer, and backcountry resource conservation manager (for the Appalachian Mountain Club, a job she held for six years). Her latest post is Vermont and New Hampshire representative for the Conservation Fund. She lives in Shelburne, New Hampshire, where she is guardian for her disabled brother and sister and where she tends eighteen sled dogs, with whom she competes in races around North America.

JONATHAN MINGLE ("The Red Squirrel and the Second Law, or, What the Caretaker Saw") has published articles on the environment, climate change, science and development in the *New York Times*, *Slate*, the *Los Angeles Times*, *Quartz*, and the *Boston Globe*. He is the author of *Fire and Ice: Soot, Solidarity and Survival on the Roof of the World*, a nonfiction narrative about black carbon pollution in the Himalaya and around the world. He is a former Middlebury Fellow in Environmental Journalism, and a graduate of the University of California, Berkeley's Energy and Resources Group.

RICK OUIMET ("The Northeast's True Hundred-Mile Wilderness?") teaches high-school English at New York City's Millennium Arts Academy, where he is weaving excerpts from Laura and Guy Waterman's *Wilderness Ethics* into his unit on Camus, Sisyphus, and Elizabeth Bishop. Referring to a story the Watermans told of a wounded Vermont butterfly that struggled southwest despite nearby birds that might have attacked, he reports, "It is no exaggeration to say the maimed monarch of East Corinth has found refuge from the peewees and phoebes—in the fertile minds of his South Bronx students!"

AARON PICCIRILLO ("Getting Lost in a Familiar Part of the Woods") is a writer and musician living in western Connecticut. He has a bachelor's degree in literature from SUNY Purchase and a master of arts degree from the University of Manchester. His master's thesis analyzed the works of D. H. Lawrence through an ecocritical lens and, since then, he has written about Western esotericism, nature, spirituality, creativity, art and literature, music, and the food industry. He has published in *Clavis* journal and is a contributing writer to the blog *Ultraculture*. His work can be viewed at forgottenforms.com.

DEVON REYNOLDS ("Steward's Story") worked several seasons as a High Peaks summit steward in the Adirondacks. She graduated from Brown University with a bachelor of arts in Africana studies and Portuguese and Brazilian studies. She studied in Brazil on a Fulbright scholarship and now is program manager for Colorado Youth at Risk.

NANCY RICH ("Walking with Our Faces to the Sun") did graduate work at Antioch University New England and teaches environmental biology at Springfield (Massachusetts) Technical Community College.

AMY SEIDL ("Foreword") is a lecturer in environmental studies at the University of Vermont and the author of two books on climate change, *Early Spring: Waking to a Warming World* (2009) and *Finding Higher Ground: Adaptation in the*

Age of Warming (2011), both from Beacon Press. In 2010, Dr. Seidl received a "Best of the Best" award for *Early Spring* from the Association of Academic and University Presses. Dr. Seidl received a PhD in ecology and evolutionary biology from the University of Vermont and a master's degree in entomology from Colorado State University. She lives in Huntington, Vermont, with her husband and two daughters.

SANDY STOTT ("Looking Up") serves as *Appalachia*'s Accidents Editor, writes for *The Roost*, the blog of the Thoreau Farm Trust, and contributes to various other publications and sites as a freelance writer. He is at work on a book about search and rescue in New Hampshire's White Mountains for University Press of New England. He lives and runs in Brunswick, Maine. A former English teacher at Concord Academy, he was editor of *Appalachia* throughout the 1990s.

BETHANY TAYLOR ("The Warp and Weft"), a native of New Hampshire, lives in Portland, Maine, and works on various environmental and writing projects. She has been delighted to be part of the Waterman Fund essay contest review panel since 2012.

LEAH TITCOMB ("Catching a Fish") is a registered Maine Guide who teaches young people about the natural world. She is often found canoeing on the waterways of Maine or adventuring in the mountains.

WENDY UNGAR ("Where the Trail Ends") is a scientist, hiker, and writer who divides her time between Toronto, Canada, and Loon Lake, New York, in the northwest Adirondacks. She has published previously in *Adirondac*, where portions of this story first appeared in 2013, and she is working on her first novel.

Born and raised in Boulder, Colorado, JENNY KELLY WAGNER ("The Cage Canyon") has worked as an experiential educator in the mountains of southern Colorado and in remote communities in West Africa. She spent the winter of 2014 living in a yurt as a full-time staff member of the Mission: Wolf sanctuary. She lived and worked in Senegal after that, and then returned to Boulder.

LAURA WATERMAN ("Letter to Readers") homesteaded for twenty-seven years in East Corinth, Vermont, with her husband, Guy Waterman, in whose memory she established the Waterman Fund after his death in 2000. She is author, with Guy, of several books, including the mountain history *Forest and Crag*

(Appalachian Mountain Books, 2003), *The Green Guide to Low-Impact Hiking and Camping* (originally *Backwoods Ethics*, The Countryman Press, 1993 and 2015), and *Wilderness Ethics* (The Countryman Press, 1993 and 2000). She is author of a memoir, *Losing the Garden: The Story of a Marriage* (Shoemaker and Hoard, 2005) and is working on a novel about the A. W. Greely expedition to the Arctic in 1881–1884. She lives in East Corinth.

MICHAEL WEJCHERT ("Epigoni, Revisited"), a writer and climber, lives in Jackson, New Hampshire. He works on the Appalachian Mountain Club's construction crew and as a climbing guide for International Mountain Climbing School in North Conway, New Hampshire. Both jobs keep him outside all day, and well-equipped to take annual trips to Alaska and South America, where he attempts to climb remote mountains with varying degrees of success.

CHRISTINE WOODSIDE ("Introduction") is the editor of *Appalachia* journal, published by the Appalachian Mountain Club. She has worked as a writer and editor since 1981 and especially likes covering environmental change and how people clash with the natural world. She thru-hiked the Appalachian Trail in 1987 and has explored the White Mountains, Maine, and Vermont high country for three decades. Her new book *Libertarians on the Prairie: Laura Ingalls Wilder, Rose Wilder Lane, and the Making of the Little House Books*, was published in 2016 by Arcade. She lives with her husband in Deep River, Connecticut, where they raised their two daughters. Visit her at chriswoodside.com.

After completing thru-hikes of both the Appalachian Trail and Pacific Crest Trail, ANGELA ZUKOWSKI ("Wilderness") enrolled in a graduate studies program at Maine College of Art in Portland, Maine. She is now a K–12 certified art educator living in the White Mountains of New Hampshire.

12/18